First World War
and Army of Occupation
War Diary
France, Belgium and Germany

18 DIVISION
Divisional Troops
Royal Army Medical Corps
55 Field Ambulance
26 July 1915 - 30 April 1919

WO95/2030/1

The Naval & Military Press Ltd
www.nmarchive.com
Published in association with The National Archives

Published by

The Naval & Military Press Ltd

Unit 10 Ridgewood Industrial Park,

Uckfield, East Sussex,

TN22 5QE England

Tel: +44 (0) 1825 749494

www.naval-military-press.com

www.nmarchive.com

This diary has been reprinted in facsimile from the original. Any imperfections are inevitably reproduced and the quality may fall short of modern type and cartographic standards.

© **Crown Copyright**
Images reproduced by permission of The National Archives, London, England, 2015.

Contents

Document type	Place/Title	Date From	Date To
Heading	WO95/2030 18 Division Divisional Troops 55 Field Ambulance July 1915-April 1919		
Heading	18th Division 55th Field Ambulance July 1915-1919 Apl		
Heading	18th Division 55th Field Ambulance Vol: I 26th July 15-31 July 15		
War Diary	Codford Salisbury	26/07/1915	26/07/1915
War Diary	Havre	27/07/1915	27/07/1915
War Diary	Coisy	28/07/1915	31/07/1915
Heading	18th Division 55th Field Ambulance Vol: II From 1-31.8.15 August 1915		
War Diary	Coisy	01/08/1915	08/08/1915
War Diary	St. Gratien	08/08/1915	22/08/1915
War Diary	Mericourt L'Abbe	23/08/1915	23/08/1915
War Diary	Mericourt	24/08/1915	31/08/1915
Miscellaneous	To report that during the night of 22/23rd inst 55 Field Ambulance moved into its allotted position		
Diagram etc			
Heading	18th Division 55th Field Ambulance Vol III. Sept. 15		
War Diary	Mericourt L'Abbe	01/09/1915	21/09/1915
War Diary	Mericourt	22/09/1915	30/09/1915
Heading	18th Division 55th Field Ambulance Vol 4 Oct 15		
War Diary	Mericourt L'Abbe	01/10/1915	13/10/1915
War Diary	Mericourt	14/10/1915	28/10/1915
War Diary	Mericourt L'Abbe	29/10/1915	31/10/1915
Heading	18th Division 55th F.A. Vol: 5 Nov. 15		
War Diary	Mericourt L'Abbe	01/11/1915	12/11/1915
War Diary	Daours	12/11/1915	30/11/1915
Heading	18th Div 55th F.A. Vol: Dec 1915		
War Diary	Daours	01/12/1915	31/12/1915
Heading	18th Div F/155/2 55th F.A. Vol: 7 Jan 1916		
War Diary	Daours	01/01/1916	12/01/1916
War Diary	Mericourt L'Abbe	13/01/1916	31/01/1916
Heading	55. F.A. 18th Div Vol. 8. Feb 1916		
War Diary	Mericourt L'Abbe	01/02/1916	05/02/1916
War Diary	Pont. Noyelles	05/02/1916	29/02/1916
Heading	18th Div 55 F amb Vol 9410 March 1916 April 1916		
War Diary	Pont. Noyelles	01/03/1916	05/03/1916
War Diary	Corbie	06/03/1916	20/03/1916
War Diary	Chipilly	20/03/1916	30/04/1916
Heading	18th Div No. 55 F. Amb. May 1916.		
War Diary	Chipilly	01/05/1916	03/05/1916
War Diary	La Houssoye	04/05/1916	04/05/1916
War Diary	Bertangles	05/05/1916	31/05/1916
Heading	No. 55 F.A. June 1916.		
War Diary	Bertangles	01/06/1916	12/06/1916
War Diary	Sailly Le Sec	13/06/1916	16/06/1916
War Diary	Grovetown	17/06/1916	24/06/1916
War Diary	L.10.C.1.1.	25/06/1916	30/06/1916
Heading	55th Field Ambulance July 1916		

Heading	A.D.M.S. 18th Division. Herewith Diary for July 1916 forwarded in accordance with 18th Div R O No 522 d/ 15/7/16		
War Diary	L.10.C.1.1.	01/07/1916	08/07/1916
War Diary	J 24	08/07/1916	14/07/1916
War Diary	Maricourt	14/07/1916	20/07/1916
War Diary	J. 24	20/07/1916	21/07/1916
War Diary	Huchenneville	21/07/1916	23/07/1916
War Diary	Campagne	24/07/1916	27/07/1916
War Diary	Le. Brearde	28/07/1916	28/07/1916
War Diary	Fletre	29/07/1916	31/07/1916
Heading	18th Div. No. 55 Field Ambulance August 1916		
War Diary	Fletre	01/08/1916	03/08/1916
War Diary	Fort Rompu	04/08/1916	22/08/1916
War Diary	Estaires	23/08/1916	24/08/1916
War Diary	Tincquette	25/08/1916	31/08/1916
Heading	18th Div. 55th Field Ambulance. Sept Oct 1916		
Heading	A.D.M.S. 18th Division. War Diary 557A for September 1916		
War Diary	Tincquette	01/09/1916	08/09/1916
War Diary	Houvin Houvigneul	09/09/1916	09/09/1916
War Diary	Lucheux	10/09/1916	10/09/1916
War Diary	Puchevillers	11/09/1916	25/09/1916
War Diary	Clairfaye Farm	25/09/1916	04/10/1916
War Diary	Fienvillers	05/10/1916	14/10/1916
War Diary	Bretel	15/10/1916	15/10/1916
War Diary	Rubempre	16/10/1916	16/10/1916
War Diary	Albert	17/10/1916	22/10/1916
War Diary	La Boiselle	23/10/1916	31/10/1916
Heading	17th Div. No. 55 Field Ambulance Nov 1916		
War Diary	La Boiselle	01/11/1916	21/11/1916
War Diary	Vadencourt	22/11/1916	22/11/1916
War Diary	Fienvillers	23/11/1916	25/11/1916
War Diary	Maison Ponthieu	26/11/1916	26/11/1916
War Diary	Domvast	27/11/1916	27/11/1916
War Diary	Abbeville Map	28/11/1916	30/11/1916
Heading	18th Div 55th Field Ambulance Dec 1916		
War Diary	Domvast	01/12/1916	31/12/1916
Heading	18th Div. 55th Field Ambulance Jan. 1917		
War Diary	Domvast	01/01/1917	11/01/1917
War Diary	Coulonvillers	12/01/1917	12/01/1917
War Diary	Le Meillard	13/01/1917	14/01/1917
War Diary	Beauquesne	15/01/1917	15/01/1917
War Diary	Forceville	16/01/1917	31/01/1917
Heading	18th Div. 55th Field Ambulance. Feb. 1917		
War Diary	Forceville	01/02/1917	21/02/1917
War Diary	Vadencourt	22/02/1917	28/02/1917
Heading	55th Field Ambulance. Mar. 1917		
War Diary	Vadencourt	01/03/1917	04/03/1917
War Diary	W.9.b.9.1	05/03/1917	12/03/1917
War Diary	R 33 Central	13/03/1917	22/03/1917
War Diary	Vadencourt	23/03/1917	23/03/1917
War Diary	Saveuse	24/03/1917	25/03/1917
War Diary	In The Train	26/03/1917	26/03/1917
War Diary	Boeseghem	27/03/1917	27/03/1917
War Diary	I3 d + b	28/03/1917	31/03/1917

Heading	18th Div. 55th F.G. April. 1917		
Miscellaneous	B.E.F. Summary of Medical War Diaries for 55th F.A. 17th Divn. 2nd Corps. 1st Army 7th Corps-3rd Army from 29/4/17. Western Front. April-May. 1917.		
War Diary	Headquarters	03/04/1917	03/04/1917
War Diary	Weather: Accommodation	03/04/1917	03/04/1917
War Diary	Moves	20/04/1917	28/04/1917
War Diary	Moves Detachment	28/04/1917	28/04/1917
War Diary	Transfer	29/04/1917	29/04/1917
War Diary	Medical Arrangements	29/04/1917	30/04/1917
War Diary	Casualties	29/04/1917	30/04/1917
War Diary	Headquarters	03/04/1917	03/04/1917
War Diary	Weather: Accommodation	03/04/1917	03/04/1917
War Diary	Moves	20/04/1917	28/04/1917
War Diary	Moves Detachment	28/04/1917	28/04/1917
War Diary	Transfer	29/04/1917	29/04/1917
War Diary	Medical Arrangements	29/04/1917	30/04/1917
War Diary	Casualties	29/04/1917	30/04/1917
War Diary	I3 d & b. (Boeseghem)	01/04/1917	19/04/1917
War Diary	Lambres	20/04/1917	20/04/1917
War Diary	Bethune	21/04/1917	27/04/1917
War Diary	Pressy Les Pernes	27/04/1917	28/04/1917
War Diary	S.2 B Central	29/04/1917	30/04/1917
Heading	18th Div No. 55. F.Q. May. 1917.		
Miscellaneous	B.E.F. Summary of Medical War Diaries For 55th F.A. 18th Divn. 2nd Corps. 1st Army 7th Corps-3rd Army from 29/4/17. Western Front. April-May. 1917.	29/04/1917	29/04/1917
War Diary	Operations	03/05/1917	03/05/1917
War Diary	Casualties	03/05/1917	03/05/1917
War Diary	Casualties R.A.M.C.	04/05/1917	04/05/1917
War Diary	Casualties	05/05/1917	05/05/1917
War Diary	Casualties R.A.M.C.	06/05/1917	06/05/1917
War Diary	Assistance	10/05/1917	10/05/1917
War Diary	Operations R.A.M.C.	17/05/1917	17/05/1917
War Diary	Operations	21/05/1917	21/05/1917
War Diary	Casualties	21/05/1917	31/05/1917
War Diary	Operations	03/05/1917	03/05/1917
War Diary	Casualties	03/05/1917	04/05/1917
War Diary	Casualties R.A.M.C.	04/05/1917	04/05/1917
War Diary	Casualties	05/05/1917	05/05/1917
War Diary	Casualties R.A.M.C.	06/05/1917	06/05/1917
War Diary	Assistance	10/05/1917	10/05/1917
War Diary	Operations R.A.M.C.	17/05/1917	17/05/1917
War Diary	Operations	21/05/1917	21/05/1917
War Diary	Casualties	21/05/1917	31/05/1917
War Diary	S.2.B Central	01/05/1917	31/05/1917
Heading	No 55 F.Q. June 1917.		
War Diary	S.2.B. Central	01/06/1917	16/06/1917
War Diary	Coigneux	17/06/1917	30/06/1917
Heading	No. 55 F.A. July 1917		
War Diary	Coigneux	01/07/1916	02/07/1916
War Diary	Caumesnil	03/07/1916	03/07/1916
War Diary	Wippenhoeke	04/07/1916	05/07/1916
War Diary	H 27 d 4.1.	06/07/1916	06/07/1916
War Diary	H 27 e. 1.9	17/07/1917	24/07/1917
War Diary	Ouderdom	25/07/1917	30/07/1917

Type	Location	Start	End
War Diary	H 27 d 4.1	31/07/1917	31/07/1917
Heading	No 55 F.A. Aug 1917		
War Diary	H 27.d. 4.1	01/08/1917	02/08/1917
War Diary	Waratah G 15.a.3.0	03/08/1917	04/08/1917
War Diary	H 27 e 1.9	05/08/1917	18/08/1917
War Diary	Blankart Farm Near Zeggers Cappel	19/08/1917	31/08/1917
Heading	No. 55 F.A. Sept 1917		
War Diary	Blankart Farm Near Zeggers Cappel	01/09/1917	22/09/1917
War Diary	Sheet 27 F. 29.d 5.9. L'Ebbe. Farm	23/09/1917	28/09/1917
War Diary	G 2.a 2.4 sheet 28	29/09/1917	30/09/1917
Heading	No. 55. F.a. Oct 1917.		
War Diary	G 2 a 2.4 Sheet 28	01/10/1917	31/10/1917
Heading	No. 55 F.A. Nov. 1917		
War Diary	Sheet 27 F 1 b 4.2	01/11/1917	03/11/1917
War Diary	B 10 e. 3.3.	04/11/1917	07/11/1917
War Diary	B 10 e 3.3. map 28	08/11/1917	27/11/1917
War Diary	B 10. e 3.3. sheet 28	28/11/1917	30/11/1917
Heading	No. 55. F.A. Dec. 1917		
War Diary	B 10 e 3.3 Sheet 28	01/12/1917	16/12/1917
War Diary	Monnecove	17/12/1917	27/12/1917
War Diary	Rousbrugge	28/12/1917	28/12/1917
War Diary	Crombeke	29/12/1917	31/12/1917
Heading	No 55. F.A. Jan. 1918		
War Diary	Crombeke	01/01/1918	27/01/1918
War Diary	W. 17. d.	28/01/1918	31/01/1918
Heading	No. 55. F.A. Feb. 1918		
War Diary	W 17 d	01/02/1918	08/02/1918
War Diary	Couarcy	09/02/1918	13/02/1918
War Diary	Tirlancourt	14/02/1918	28/02/1918
Heading	55th Field Ambulance. Mar 1918.		
War Diary	Tirlancourt	01/03/1918	23/03/1918
War Diary	Lagny	24/03/1918	26/03/1918
War Diary	Compiegne	27/03/1918	31/03/1918
Heading	55th Field Ambulance. Apr. 1918.		
War Diary		01/04/1918	02/04/1918
War Diary	Amiens.	03/04/1918	19/04/1918
War Diary	Longpre	20/04/1918	28/04/1918
War Diary	Montigny	29/04/1918	30/04/1918
Miscellaneous	Claim for Indemnification-Officers.	21/04/1918	21/04/1918
Miscellaneous	Claim for Indemnification-Officers.		
Miscellaneous	18th Div. No. Q. 319 Subject:- Indemnification Claims, Officers. 53rd Inf. Bde.	02/05/1918	02/05/1918
Miscellaneous	10 Essex/Forwarded	03/05/1918	03/05/1918
Miscellaneous	O.C. 10th (S) Bn. The Essex Regt.	04/05/1918	04/05/1918
Heading	No. 55 F.A. May 1918.		
War Diary	Franvillers	01/05/1918	24/05/1918
War Diary	B.15 b.	25/05/1918	31/05/1918
Miscellaneous	18th Division	07/05/1918	07/05/1918
Miscellaneous	A Form Messages And Signals.	11/05/1918	11/05/1918
Miscellaneous	Headquarters, 18th Division.	09/05/1918	09/05/1918
Heading	55th F.A. June 1918.		
War Diary	Vadencourt	01/06/1918	30/06/1918
Heading	No. 55. F.A. July 1918.		
War Diary	Vadencourt	01/07/1918	12/07/1918
War Diary	Dreuil Les Molliens.	13/07/1918	30/07/1918
War Diary	Frechen Court.	31/07/1918	31/07/1918

Type	Description	Start	End
Heading	No. 55 F. Amb. Aug. 1918.		
War Diary	Frechen Court	01/08/1918	02/08/1918
War Diary	Montigny	03/08/1918	19/08/1918
War Diary	Bonnay	20/08/1918	27/08/1918
War Diary	E 18 b 2.8	28/08/1918	30/08/1918
War Diary	A 21a 8.9.	31/08/1918	31/08/1918
Heading	55th F.A. Sept. 1918		
War Diary	A. 21 a. 8.9	01/09/1918	07/09/1918
War Diary	D 20 c Central 62 e sheet	08/09/1918	18/09/1918
War Diary	D 20 c Central	19/09/1918	22/09/1918
War Diary	C 17 d 7.9.	23/09/1918	25/09/1918
War Diary	Combles	26/09/1918	27/09/1918
War Diary	St. Emilie	28/09/1918	30/09/1918
Operation(al) Order(s)	55 Field Ambulance Orders No. 1.	28/09/1918	28/09/1918
Heading	No. 55 F.A. Oct. 1918		
War Diary	St Emilie	01/10/1918	01/10/1918
War Diary	Vadencourt	02/10/1918	17/10/1918
War Diary	Templeux La Fosse	18/10/1918	18/10/1918
War Diary	Beaurevoir	19/10/1918	19/10/1918
War Diary	Elincourt	20/10/1918	20/10/1918
War Diary	Maurois	21/10/1918	21/10/1918
War Diary	Reumont	22/10/1918	22/10/1918
War Diary	Le Cateau	22/10/1918	24/10/1918
War Diary	Forest	25/10/1918	31/10/1918
Miscellaneous	Operation 18 Division 23/10/18 to 27/10/18.	27/10/1918	27/10/1918
Heading	No 55 F.A. Nov. 1918		
War Diary	Le Forest	01/11/1918	03/11/1918
War Diary	Bousies	04/11/1918	07/11/1918
War Diary	Pommereuil	08/11/1918	12/11/1918
War Diary	Elincourt	13/11/1918	30/11/1918
Heading	No 55 F.A. Dec. 1918		
War Diary	Elincourt	01/12/1918	31/12/1918
Heading	18 Div No 55 Field Ambulance Jan. 1919		
War Diary	Elincourt	01/01/1919	19/01/1919
War Diary	Ligny	20/01/1919	27/01/1919
War Diary	Ligny-En-Cambresis.	28/01/1919	31/01/1919
Heading	55 F.A. Apr. 1919		
War Diary	Ligny	01/04/1919	30/04/1919

WO 95/2030

(1)
18 Division
Divisional Troops
55 Field Ambulance
July 1915 – April 1919

18TH DIVISION

55TH FIELD AMBULANCE

JUN 1915 - ~~DEC 1918~~
1919 APL

121/6300

121/6300/18 — 1/4/17 5th Division

55th Field Ambulance

Vol: I

26th July 115 —
31st "

A.D.S. Hart

Army Form C. 2118

WAR DIARY 55: Field Ambulance

INTELLIGENCE SUMMARY

(Erase heading not required.)

Instructions regarding War Diaries and Intelligence Summaries are contained in F.S. Regs., Part II. and the Staff Manual respectively. Title Pages will be prepared in manuscript.

Place	Date	Hour	Summary of Events and Information	Remarks and references to Appendices
Codford St Mary	26.7.15		Entrained at WYLYE for SOUTHAMPTON.	
HAVRE	27.7.15	6.30 p.m	Arrived Havre 6.30 p.m	
	28.7.15		Disentrained LONGUEAU near AMIENS (sheet 12) arrived and billeted (1.30 p.m.) Highland until 10.0 a.m. Had our steam	
	29.7.15	10.0 a.m	2nd F.A.M. HOLDING R.A.M.C. 55Fd and marched last night with instructions to Council clearing station opened dressing station in a barn owing to lack of large houses or rooms in village, took over the suitable accommodation	
	30.7.15		but to be found.	
	31.7.15		One aluminium in room three. Later, evacuated sick to H.C.C.S. this morning. A 34.	

121/6607

11 18th Division

55th Field Ambulance

Vol: II

From 1 - 31. 8. 15

August 1915

WAR DIARY 55th Ambulance
INTELLIGENCE SUMMARY

Army Form C. 2118

Place	Date	Hour	Summary of Events and Information	Remarks and references to Appendices
CO. 1SY	1.8.15		7 cases evacuated (4 remained, 6 admitted) one remaining A.34. Being in Brigade who H.Q. Brigade sent for same which then were to render RD in HQ and call on this unit for same. This causing unnecessary clerical labor, as the unit whose Divisional returns direct Brigade HQ officer to know this, but as the order is transmitted, it must be complied with.	A/Winder
"	2.8.15		F. & J. YATES. R.A.M.C. attd 84 Bde R.F.A. admitted unit influenza. Hy. notified. Batteries 4 remaining. A.34. Imperial R.A.C. medical arrangements by order of A.D.M.S. Invitation to army commander of Brigade camp. Cancelled owing to weather. Info received by private wire.	
"	3.8.15		Rain. 4 remaining. 6 admitted. 4 to duty. 3 to CCS. 3 remaining. F & J YATES convalescent I.A.34.	
"	4.8.15		Stationary. admitted 4. remaining 2. To CCS 5. Et YATES to duty. A.34.	
"	5.8.15		admitted 2. to CCS 1. remaining 1. Infantile B 808 3rd Army of 55 R die ynot	
"	6.8.15	7.0.p.m	admitted 1. to CCS 1. remaining 1. R same Division recommissioning 55th H/F Ble to how bittel area LA NEUVILLE - BONNAY - LA HOUSSOYE hence much ordered had to O.C became 9.0 am	
"	7.8.15		S/Sgt LIND & S/Sgt ads R.F.A. admitted to hospital 85 Ambulance at - Trufurny to CCS. continuum 55 F/A Ble in convoy sent in case and by temperatures came away	
"	8.8.15		Proceeded to LE HARGILL. Open division. Diary and all documents & seven stamp handed to LE HARGILL to be kept in the division.	
ST GRATIEN	8.8.15		Proceeded in charge of Hdqtrs 55 Fd Amb. to ST. GRATIEN arriving 4.30 p.m. at Chateau in company with Hdqtrs 54 Fd Amb. & Hdqtrs 56 Fd Amb. In pursuance of orders from A.D.M.S. Opened Dressing station in a temporary Hospital in the School opposite the CHURCH. 6.30.p.m. N.C.A. Admitted 16 cases. Reported to A.D.M.S. by motor cyclist messenger.	

Army Form C. 2118

WAR DIARY
or
INTELLIGENCE SUMMARY

(Erase heading not required.)

55 Fd Amb

Place	Date	Hour	Summary of Events and Information	Remarks and references to Appendices
ST. GRATIEN	9.9.15		Wylu. Range. Evacuated six cases to C.C.S. Seven to Duty. Admitted four. Remaining seven. Sent forward two F.M.P.s to Beaver. Unable to obtain Reserve Rations for Sick as indented for from Div. Supply Column — so forced to draw 40 Rations from 56 Fd Amb. One man 85 Bde R.F.A. admitted 8.30 p.m. with alleged acc. dental puncture of perineum, however probably local heavy bruising from evening lights on and a half. Eggs — milk — brandy — butter.	h.A.
do.	10.8.15		Evacuated three cases to C.C.S. four to Duty. Admitted three. Remaining seven. Received orders from A.D.M.S. to move Hospital from the School and decided to re-establish in a stable/barn attached to the Chateau on the best in sanitary place in the Village.	h.A.
do.	11.8.15		Wylu. Range. Evacuated two cases to C.C.S. two to Duty. Admitted two. Remaining nine. Proceeded to clean up stable/barn to render it habitable as a hospital. On the morning informed by Billeting Officer that School not required till Sept. 25. So had that I could remain there. Magi hindoo Rawl. not cavd. back from with S/M Turnu and R.M.S. Hawkins for Bearer Division and returned to turn with experience of Trench evacuation of casualties instruction and experience.	h.A.
do.	12.9.15		Evacuated two C.C.S. three to Duty. Admitted five. Remaining 7. hund A.D.M.S. re Evacuating School - received permission to remain in occupation. Cpl. Hawson of this unit Aerowith ill with Ptomaine poisoning suspected to have been caused by eating Confectionary obtained from a street vender - a middle aged French woman with a 2 children should cert. Admitted six. Link W.E. NIELD of 1st Royal Fusiliers has admitted	h.A.
do.	13.9.15		Evacuated five C.C.S. three to Duty. Admitted six to No 5. C.C.S. Remaining five. An anaesthetic (CHCl3) was given to a man for perfect removing a buried stump of molar. Owing to the fact that No 929 J. army description suffering from jaundice and very considerable difficulty was experienced with the anaesthetic. the whole stump and very considerable difficulty was experienced with the anaesthetic.	h.A.

1875 Wt. W593/826 1,000,000 4/15 J.B.C. & A. A.D.S.S./Forms/C. 2118.

WAR DIARY or INTELLIGENCE SUMMARY

Army Form C. 2118

Vol II
map/12

55 Fd Amb

Place	Date	Hour	Summary of Events and Information	Remarks and references to Appendices
ST. GRATIEN	14.8.15		Evacuated twelve to C.C.S.; One to Duty; Admitted twentyfive; Remaining seventeen.	
"	15.8.15		Returned to Headquarters after visits. Line which 15 Fd Ambulance is working is reported to A.D.M.S. Line FRICOURT-CARNOY-MARICOURT-VAUX maps 12 & 13. Parties of stretcher bearers have been sent out for 3 days at a time, with the bearers of 15 Fd Amb for instruction. 3 cases evacuated to H.E.E.s.	Appendices
"	16.8.15		Brigadier another JEAN de ST QUENTIN admitted, suffering from fall in aeroplane, fractures & wounds, drained and sent to AMIENS French evacuation hospital. Bearers evacuated to etc CORBIE 5 to Divisional stationary DAOURS.	Report Report
"	17.8.15		4 evacuated to H.E.Es. 5 to Div rest. Bearers moved from ETINEHEM to CHIPILLY 1.30 p.m. Orders of A.D.M.S. 5th Division. Report received and transmitted to A.D.M.S. 18th Division.	Report
"	18.8.15		Drew stores from Adv Med Store BEAUVAL. Accompanied D.A.D.M.S. to choose site for dressing station at MÉAULTE and MERICOURT. One heavy draught horse to veterinary hospital.	Report
"	19.8.15		Proceeded to BRAY to choose dressing station in area allotted to 53rd Fd Amb only suitable site is that occupied by 15 Fd Amb, who are moving into the building. Reported this building to A.D.M.S.	Report
"	20.8.15 21.8.15 22.8.15		TO MERICOURT. Lt. CLARKE R.A.M.C attached to D.A.D.M.S. to reconnoitre main dressing station on a farm set about had been filled of with gas. Lt. CLARKE R.A.M.C S.R. 75th Divsn 4t. 7d Amb left. Lt. BRAME S.R joined from 54 Fd Amb. Ambulance will be down reserve F.A. 4 hours from CHIPILLY, leaves from CHIPILLY in the night 22/23 moving at 7.0 pm TO MERICOURT for main dressing station. To BRAY (SS sect) MÉAULTE (e sect) as advanced dressing stations reported ready at 10.0 am to A.D.M.S.	
MERICOURT L'ABBÉ	23.8.15		Detailed report attached. Two HD horses to Veterinary Hospital. Also one mule on 22.8. HD horse sent 18th is evacuated & indent for new horse to replace, submitted.	Appendix 1 Report

Army Form C. 2118

WAR DIARY
or
INTELLIGENCE SUMMARY

(Erase heading not required.)

5·5 Fd Amb

Instructions regarding War Diaries and Intelligence Summaries are contained in F. S. Regs., Part II. and the Staff Manual respectively. Title Pages will be prepared in manuscript.

Place	Date	Hour	Summary of Events and Information	Remarks and references to Appendices
MERICOURT	24.8.15		5 Wounded and severe during previous 24 hours. In all 9 evacuated to e.e.s. 17 to div Rest.	[sgd]
"	25.8.15		12 wounded two severe during previous 24 hours. To e.e.s. 16 to D.R. 12 - one officer Lieut OSBORNE rich evacuated to e.e.s.	[sgd]
"	26.8.15		# No 1750 Pte CHANDLER. 9. 8th R Surrey (Reg.) admitted 2.15 pm 25th bullet wound abdomen died 6.30 pm same day. necessary action taken. 4 wounded to e.e.s. 5 sick, 10 in to div Rest. 2 Lt BURCHELL A.S.C. 18th Div Suppl to Div Rest Influenza. One case shown e.e.s. in case of cerebrosperinomenyst 10th Essex Regt. D.D.M.S. 3rd army inspected. Paid 3.8/30 centimes for water barrels & planks for advanced well string posts at BRAY as water has to be carried at night. Paid 8.75 francs for 7 litres methylated spirit as the supply in advanced and supply officers pack certificate of none available. 15 cases to e.e.s. including 3 wounded 8 sick to Div Rest grassed and fined upon as necessary wound made. Capt BRADISH R.A.M.C. reported for duty.	[sgd]
"	27.8.15			[sgd]
"	28.8.15		28 cases to e.e.s. including 15 wounded 4 to div rest Two officers Lt SKINNER 7 R W Kent evacuated to 2 Lt DALTON 10th Essex Influenza transferred to e.e.s. No 12480 Pte GILLIAM E. 6th R Berks R.t died at Ad D. Statn BRAY. multiple wounds (shell). necessary action taken. Paid through inspect 22.50 franc for him. Retaining room for expertise.	[sgd]
"	29.8.15		evacuated 22 cases and one officer 2 Lt TALBOT RS to e.e.s. 3 to Div Rest. (6 wounded + office) 2 returned. No 37013 Pte HART. A 55 Vlant. (Eymouth) (inc III.) gassed by mine explosion C.O. 15 evain. local purchase 5 litres methylated spirit 6.25 pr. 2dm ess 4.80 pr. 5 litre milk 1 fr. with accommodation for 250 stretchers or 500 sitters.	[sgd]

WAR DIARY or INTELLIGENCE SUMMARY

Army Form C. 2118

Vol II

5 5 Fd Ambulance

(Erase heading not required.)

Place	Date	Hour	Summary of Events and Information	Remarks and references to Appendices
MERICOURT	30.8.15		Evacuated 19 including 3 wounded to C.C.S. were invalided 7 cases of influenza from Australians. 6 to Divisional Rest.	Appx
"	31.8.15		Evacuated 120 including 9 wounded to C.C.S. also 1 officer Capt. C.W. HEMP 6 R Fus Regt wound face + injured eyes. 4 to divisional rest. Arranged with 9 u e 53 by side for an ambulance motor to evacuate any wounded at CITADEL from GRAY. = daylight, leaving Carrefour about 10 pm instead of waiting till day.	Appx
"		9.15h	No 17060 P.G. PRITLIT/H. A 8th Argyll + Sutherland shaped back + stayed. We did so from 8 to 12 noon	Appx

To report that during the night of 22/23rd inst 55 Field Ambulance moved into it's allotted position.

"B" Section Tent subdivision has formed an advance dressing station at BRAY in the second house on the right hand side of the Rue de Corbie, this being the main CORBIE – BRAY road leading into the town.

The R.A.M.C. personnel of this advance dressing station consists of 2 Officers and 37 Other ranks. The house taken gives sufficient accommodation for cases awaiting evacuation to main dressing station.

There is also accommodation for necessary transport in a yard.

"C" Section tent subdivision has formed an advance dressing station at MEAULTE situated on southern side of road fork at western end of village. It consists of several small rooms, not very suitable but sufficient to deal with cases until evacuated to main dressing station.

There is better accommodation available in the village but being in the vicinity of the Church, which affords

2/ a landmark for shell fire, it was decided to occupy the building chosen.

The RAMC Personnel consists of 3 officers and 53 other Ranks who are billeted in barns etc. in the immediate vicinity.

The transport is parked under trees opposite dressing station and the horses are in the immediate rear of the dressing station amongst trees.

Evacuations

BRAY. Cars can run at night to CITADEL where 8 men and 1 N.C.O. are stationed to bring down cases from Regimental Aid Posts. A similar arrangement holds at BRONFAY.

MÉAULTE. Cars can run at night as far as the bridge near point 54 half inch north of 'E' in BÉCORDEL. Cases are brought down to this point from Regimental Aid Post by bearers belonging to the Field Ambulance, squads going up every night and staying in Regimental Aid Post. Cases can be evacuated in daytime by means of a track running roughly parallel to the BÉCORDEL BECOURT - MÉAULTE road

3/ partly by hand carriage & partly by motor ambulance, cases being brought to a cottage at BECORDEL-BECOURT. It may be desirable to establish a collecting station at this village but the Advance Dressing Stn. is to report on this matter.

Instructions have been given that in the event of the dressing Stn. being shelled cases are to be placed in the fields half mile west and sufficient personnel left to deal with casualties in the village.

The Main dressing Station has been established at MERICOURT at the western end of the village. A dispensary and dressing room has been opened at the "school" house on right hand side of the CORBIE-MERICOURT Road immediately after entering the town. A ward capable of accommodating 80 or more cases has been prepared off the road turning to left opposite the dispensary (see sketch map). As soon as available a large well built barn opposite the dispensary will be opened in lieu of the present ward. The R&MC personnel consists of 8 officers and 92 other

4/ ranks billeted near the ward now occupied.

The transport is parked among trees & in rear of mens billets and the motor ambulances under cover in front of the billets.

Transport at each advance dressing stn. consists of 1 water cart, one medical store cart and one G.S. wagon for stores. The remainder of the horse transport is at the main dressing stn. Motor Transport. One heavy car (Talbot) and one light car (Ford) is stationed at BRAY and two heavy cars (Talbot) at MÉAULTE. A car from H.Q. proceeds to each ADS every evening with rations for the ensuing day and collects cases awaiting evacuation to the main dressing stn. Cars will be sent up at other times as found necessary. Advance D.S. have instructions that all cases for evacuation must reach the main dressing stn. by 9 am. to enable evacuations to D.R. or C.C.S. to be carried out as a routine measure at 10.30 am.

5/ When two further motor cycles are received it is proposed to place one at each ADS to complete the chain of communication.

It may prove necessary to alter the above arrangements after experience in working

M/Winder.
Major RAMC
OC 56 Field Ambce

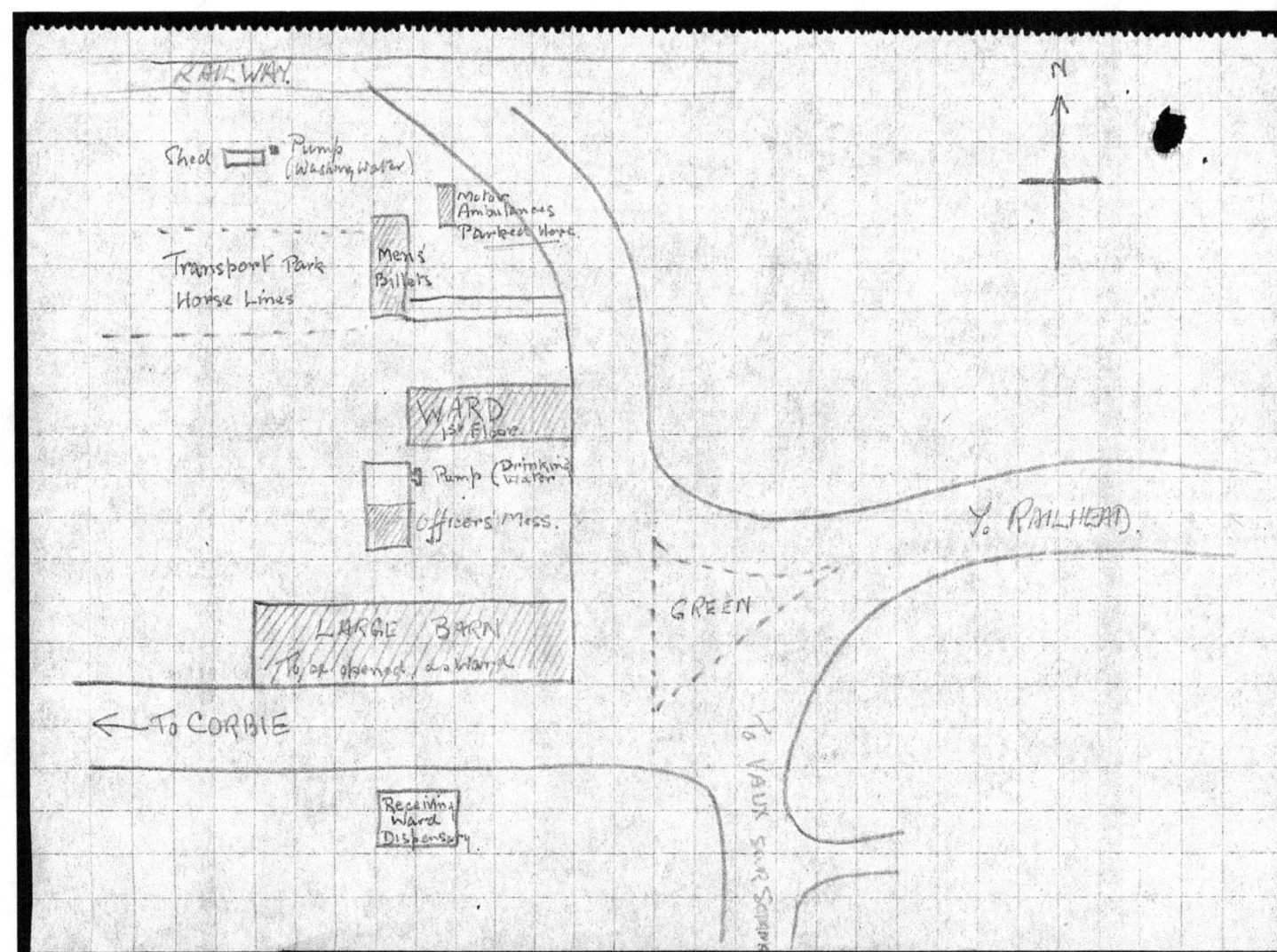

121/6971

18th Division

No. 55th Field Ambulance
Vol III

Sept. 15

Sept 15

WAR DIARY or INTELLIGENCE SUMMARY

Army Form C. 2118

Vol 3

55 7d And.

September

Place	Date	Hour	Summary of Events and Information	Remarks and references to Appendices
MERICOURT L'ABBE	1.9.15		22 cases evacuated to C.C.S. 20 wounded with 1 death. Pte Pretty & hopefully shown in diary 31.8.15. 7th divisional set.	
"	2.9.15		14 cases including 6 wounded to C.C.S. 10 to divisional set. Two officers 7.2 Kent R Capt HOBBES H. Shell following concussion to C.C.S. Lieut PRATT. D.B. 5537d And retained for treatment. Pte PRETTY. 8th hopefully buried.	
"	3.9.15		11 cases to C.C.S. including 6 wounded in actn. 6th D. Rat. No 1972 Pte HAWKINS A.H. 7.2 Kent R died 3.0 pm & buried 1.9.15 admitted 1.9.15 died 3.0 hrs 2 officers buried and MERICOURT. No 3204 Pte WRIGHT. 99/758 150 hrs and 8 wounded. CITADEL. Buried near ___ 3rd int Lieut PRATT. RAMC 55rd and to duty, evacuated 12 to C.C.S. including 6 wounded. 12th D. Rat.	
"	4.9.15			
"	5.9.15		Evacuated 8 to C.C.S. including 5 wounded. 19th Div Rat. 2 cases wounded self-inflicted, returned units notified.	
"	6.9.15		Evacuated 8 to C.C.S. including 3 wounded. 13th D. rat. mild 3 Litre 60 a. asp 18 - 360/1 for period 1-7th had through input.	
"	7.9.15		Evacuated 19 to C.C.S. including 4 wounded. 15th D. rat. Two officers 24 & 1 777 F.R.O 10th mon & major FLETCHER. W.R. hopeful to no C.C.S. 1.th A7D.	
"	8.9.15		Evacuated 5 to C.C.S. 3 wounded. 15th Div Rat. Two officers to C.C.S. Lt RESTALL 12th Middlesex, bronchitis. Capt JOYCE 15 A7H machine gunner. S.S.W. buttocks arm.	
"	9.9.15		Evacuated 17 to C.C.S. including 12 wounded 4th D.rat. Two officers N.Y.O No 8110 P C.O. RAKE 11th R.7. G.S.W. knee (shell) died in amb. waggon before reaching BRAY	
"	10.9.15			

WAR DIARY or INTELLIGENCE SUMMARY

Army Form C. 2118
Vol 3

3/57d Amb

Place	Date	Hour	Summary of Events and Information	Remarks and references to Appendices
MERICOURT L'ABBE	11.9.15		Evacuated 9 to C.C.S. including 4 wounded. 10th Div Regt. Also two officers to C.C.S. Airlifted that 667 and will be attached for instructions from 12.9.15 to 30.9.15 minimum also 5 days training.	
"	12.9.15		6 to C.C.S. including 4 wounded. 18th Div Regt. 10 officers to C.C.S. 5 off & 67 other ranks evacuated this for instruction in 10th Divn including 2 officers, one 1st SPENCER Rgt.	
"	13.9.15		17 to C.C.S. including 11 wounded. 12 to D Regt. 3 officers 2 sick, one 1st SPENCER Rgt. 8 S.W. head to C.C.S. Paid 1 frame will a 4 8th pr eggs local purchase week ending 13.9.15	
"	14.9.15		4 evac to C.C.S. including 3 wounded 15 to Div Regt. Also two officers to Div Regt one Capt SILVER 8 Suffolk arrived here with no documents a not reporting sick, on communication with Brigade information was received that this man by mind M Brigadier & with approval of Divisional. Copy of correspondence taken to ADMS office & DADMS had no information and will make enquiring. Capt WATSON. 6 6 989 Pte PARSONS 8th R Sussex (canos) died 6.30 pm at A.D Station BRAY 8 SW life thigh with internal haemorrhage	
"	15.9.15		10 to C.C.S. including 5 wounded. 15 to Div Regt. visited BRAY yesterday to choose alternative site for ADS (order from ADMS) refuted suitable site 150 yds down road below present ADS on right hand side, convenient for evacuation S or W, & having a barn with ample accommodation.	
"	16.9.15		To C.C.S. 19 including 13 wounded. to D.R.18. one officer Capt HABELER. 7th R W Surrey 1 leg torn off below knee, conf t R thigh sent oates to A.D.S. BRAY & from ADS. MEAULTE. 2 Lt HERVEY 8 R Sussex S.W. hurt by transport to C.C.S. CORBIE. ADS at MEAULTE 12.10 midnight 16/17 necessary a stretcher no 1584 & " PITMAN 6th R Hants died 5.30 pm 15 S.W. R ad.	

WAR DIARY
or
INTELLIGENCE SUMMARY 55th Fd Amb

Army Form C. 2118

Vol 3

Map 12

Place	Date	Hour	Summary of Events and Information	Remarks and references to Appendices
HERICOURT LODGE	16.9.15	1.30pm	Ordered to obtain A.D. Station BRAY. Took out first personnel to complete A.D. station for ALBERT consisting 2 officers & 27 other ranks RAMC, together with full medical equipment etc from BRAY. Station at ALBERT NE end of RUE de BAPAUME. Have personned BRAY 1 officer 21 other ranks RAMC with equipment etc from Headquarters together with a bon of extra dressings etc. Reported arrangements complete at 7.0 pm to A.D.M.S.	[sig]
"	17.9.15		4 to ees including 1 wounded. 11 to D Rest. 1 officer to ees. sprain knee. No 1 BEALE had 3.0pm lt at Citadel BRAY.	[sig]
"	18.9.15		Checked up hand communication ALBERT to BECOURT on now section, trench is traversed every few yards, night angles, informally that the work and cases will have to be evacuated through BECORDEL-BECOURT to MEAULTE. 10 ff + n ees, 9 from Becourt to ees includ 2 T.D.R. including 2 even slight C.O.s. 1 case C.O. with hern elta retained. 14 925 Pte MANN 10th Essex died 1.30pm G.S.W. head.	[sig]
"	19.9.15		One officer 4 TD to ees. 9 to ees includg 2 wounded 17 to Div Rest.	[sig]
"	20.9.15		One officer + 19 OR retained for treatment 10 to ees including 4 wounded, 12 OD R. One officer with our men from ALBERT to reinforce personnel at MEAULTE, it appearing that one officer is sufficient for A.D.S. ALBERT. Notification that same extra equipment & equipment that cannot be taken at short notice will be stored in large barn at MERLEG URT.	[sig]
"	21.9.15		Stood by done 14 - 21st ees 3.60 P milk 20 p. officer yesterday displayed to bts 11 cases included. 8 wounded 4 to Div Rest. One case meningitis. Three sent T Ees & Salisburys 18th O.H. drew rations for 6 enlisting & 1 Minister to H.E.C.S. Whilst station indented for 29.7 arrived 20/15.	[sig]

30/5/15 W.t. W.593/826 1,000,000 4/15 J.B.C.& A. A.D.S.S./Forms/C. 2118.

WAR DIARY
or
INTELLIGENCE SUMMARY 55 Fd Amb

Army Form C. 2118
Vol 3
W W Winder

(Erase heading not required.)

Place	Date	Hour	Summary of Events and Information	Remarks and references to Appendices
MERICOURT	22.9.15		No 12496 L/Cpl EVANS 6* Berks Regt G.S.W. head & body died MEAULTE 5 pm 21.9.15. No 7682 Cpl STEEL 11* R Fusiliers G.S.W. leg died BRAY 5.40 pm 21/9/15. 16 evacs to C.C.S. including 10 wounded. 8 to Div Rest. 1 officer wounded to C.C.S. 1 inch. to Div Rest.	
"	23.9.15		No 7210 L/Cpl B. COLLINS 11* R Fusiliers G.S.W. Head died BRAY at 9.45 am. 12 evacs to C.C.S. including 6 wounded 16 to D Rest also one officer to D Rest. 7 S.M. on Pte BEAVIS - DALTON self inflicted wound but quiet.	
"	24.9.15		one officer to C.C.S. sick. 7 to C.C.S. 5 including 3 wounded 5 to Div Rest. Bain	
"	25.9.15		2 officers 1 wounded to C.C.S. 2 off wounded to DR to C.C.S. 9 including 5 wounded 13 D. Rest. Rain.	
"	26.9.15		7 evacs to C.C.S. including 4 wounded. 16 to Div Rest. S.M. HOARE A.D.M.S 82 nd Bde DIED shrapnel flesh at REEORDEL-RECOURT collecting post 25/9/15.	
"	27.9.15		Two officers sick to C.C.S. 16 evacs to C.C.S. including 9 wounded. 7 to Div Rest. 3 officers sick. one Lieut KEANE 55 Fd Amb to C.C.S. appendicitis. 2 to D in Rest.	
"	28.9.15		C.O. 7 evacs to C.C.S. including 2 wounded. 6 to D in Rest. Orders from A.D.M.S. for advanced dressing "stn" ALBERT to be relieved from by 56 Fd Amb. necessary arron taken.	
"	29.9.15		To C.C.S. 43 including 14 wounded. No 1873 Pte HAMMOND 7* R eents died MEAULTE G.S.W. head.	
"	30.9.15		Completed what laid out might an evacuation of wounded between points 99 - 106 & reported to A.D.M.S. Paid 1.60 h a Gg. 1 h amb for period to 30th Sept. Trench mortar 16 evacs to C.C.S. 5 to bowel event Camp HEILLY. 1 officer to reg. sick. Period 31.8 noon to 30.9 noon there were 39 admission officers (4 wounded) other ranks (232 wounded of which 13 were self inflicted)	

867

121/7593

18th Hussars

55th Field Ambulance
Vol 4
Oct 15

WAR DIARY
or
INTELLIGENCE SUMMARY

Army Form C. 2118

55th Amb Vol 4

Place	Date	Hour	Summary of Events and Information	Remarks and references to Appendices
MERICOURT L'ABBÉ	1.10.15		3 officers sick to C.C.S. Lt CUTHBERT 55/Fd Amb injuria 30.9.15. 18 cases to C.C.S. including 8 wounded. 8 to Convalescent Camp No 1918 Pte JUDGE 7 E Kent Regt died NDAUITE 3.0 pm 30th B.S.W. head No 14885 Pte PITT 7 Bedford Regt died BECORDEL-BECOURT 10 pm 30th Fracture of skull	
"	2.10.15		Lt CUTHBERT to C.C.S. Two officers wounded to C.C.S. Seven cases to C.C.S. including 6 wounded. 11 to Convalescent Camp	
"	3.10.15		1 officer wounded to C.C.S. 11 cases to C.C.S. including 6 wounded. 3 to Convey	
"	4.10.15		Two officers sick to C.C.S. 8 to C.C.S. including 3 wounded 2 to Convey. ADMS 1 x entp + DMS 3rd army inspected	
"	5.10.15		10 men wounded to C.C.S. 12 to C.C.S. including 6 wounded. 24 to Div Rest. Ravin	
"	6.10.15		8 to C.C.S. including 1 wounded. 13 to Div Rest	
"	7.10.15		34 to C.C.S. including 31 wounded. 11 to Div Rest. 1 officer wounded to C.C.S. Pd 10 sommes 2552 a .6 pr inch for minoid L.G.R. moved from barn to new hut hut up by U.S. outside chateau as a room in chateau accommodation insufficient	
"	8.10.15		1 officer wounded to C.C.S. Nine cases to C.C.S. including 6 wounded. 26 to Div Rest No 226.8 Pte CHANNON 7th RW Regt died BECORDEL-BECOURT. G.S.W. head. Further immediate accommodation for patients provided + more arranged for	
"	9.10.15		Two officers sick to C.C.S.	
"	10.10.15		1 officer sick to Div Rest. 7 to C.C.S. seven to C.C.S. including 4 wounded 7 to Div Rest	
"	11.10.15		1 sick officer to C.C.S. 10 to C.C.S. including 2 wounded 9 to Div Rest	
"	12.10.15		Two sick officers to C.C.S. 8 to C.C.S. including 7 wounded. 8 to Div Rest	
"	13.10.15		8 to C.C.S. including 2 wounded 10 to Div Rest No 9/2635 Pte RICHARDS 2/R Sussex Regt died NEAVITE G.S.W. head	

WAR DIARY or INTELLIGENCE SUMMARY

Army Form C. 2118

55 Fd Amb

Instructions regarding War Diaries and Intelligence Summaries are contained in F.S. Regs., Part II. and the Staff Manual respectively. Title Pages will be prepared in manuscript.

(Erase heading not required.)

Place	Date	Hour	Summary of Events and Information	Remarks and references to Appendices
MERICOURT	14.10.15		One officer sick to Div Rest. 16 cases to ees including 10 wounded, 10 to Div Rest. no 1806 Pte LAWRENCE W. 7 R W Surrey Regt died MEAULTE G.S.W. head. 2 Lt PRATT. DSO & supper struck of strength of unit.	appx
"	15.10.15		6 wounded, 11 cases to ees including no 2338 Pte FRY E.R.A. 7 R W Kent R died MEAULTE G.S.W. head.	appx
"	16.10.15		11 cases to ees including 4 wounded 13 to Div Rest	appx
"	17.10.15		13 cases to ees including 7 wounded 15 to Div Rest	appx
"	18.10.15		1 officer wounded to ees. 6 O.R. to Rest. no 1578 L/Cpl BRAIN 7 R W Surrey Regt. died MEAULTE G.S.W. abdomen	appx
"	19.10.15		5 to ees. including 4 wounded 8 to Div Rest. Capt R.H. SUTHERLAND RAMC. T.C. reported for duty 18th. Lt P.L.W. WILLIAMS. R.A.M.C. T.C for duty 15th	appx
"	20.10.15		7 to ees including 3 wounded 17 to Div Rest	appx
"	21.10.15		Paid 110 fr for milk ergs 3 officers sick to ees. 11 cases to ees including 8 wounded 17 to Div Rest	appx
"	22.10.15		1 officer wounded to ees. 10 O.R wounded to ees. 14 to Div Rest. no 2857 Pte PRICE J. 12 Middlesex died MEAULTE 21.10.15 G.S.W. multiple	appx
"	23.10.15		8 cases to ees including 6 wounded 5 to Div Rest	appx
"	24.10.15		1 officer sick to ees. 9 O.R. including 3 wounded, 13 O.R. to Div Rest	appx
"	25.10.15		1 officer sick to ees. 4 O.R to ees including 2 wounded 10 to Div Rest	appx
"	26.10.15		1 officer sick to ees. 10 O.R. to ees including 4 wounded 5 to Div Rest	appx
"	27.10.15		1 officer sick to ees. 11 O.R to ees including 7 wounded 8 to Div Rest. Sir Alwin Thompson consulting surgeon and [?] visited to MEAULTE	appx
"	28.10.15		no 2627 Pte DICKS. G. 8 Surrey Regt died MEAULTE 27.10. G.S.W. chest	appx

Army Form C.2118
Vol 4

WAR DIARY
or
INTELLIGENCE SUMMARY

55 Fd Amb
Infantry Division

(Erase heading not required.)

Place	Date	Hour	Summary of Events and Information	Remarks and references to Appendices
MERICOURT L'ABBE	29.10.15		1 Officer rich to C.C.S. 4 O.R. included 10 to D.R. No 10293 Pte COX 6 R. Berks died MEAULTE 1.15am 2 S.W. chest No 10001 Pte DARBY 8th Suffolk " MERICOURT 1.30pm 28 S.W. back	[initials]
"	30.10.15		1 Officer sick to C.C.S. 16 O.R. includg 11 wounded 10 to Div Rest	[initials]
"	31.10.15		1 Officer wounded to C.C.S. 19 O.R. includg 13 wounded 10 to Div Rest No 2212 Pte ROOKE 7 R.W.Surrey died MEAULTE 5.40pm 30.10.15 S.W. head Paid 12 June for BEF for period ending 31.10.15.	[initials] [initials]

55½ Z.a.
vol. 5

121/7693

18th Hussain

Nov. 15

Nov 1915

Army Form C. 2118

WAR DIARY
INTELLIGENCE SUMMARY
(Erase heading not required.)

557th Amb. Vol 5
M/Minster

Instructions regarding War Diaries and Intelligence Summaries are contained in F.S. Regs., Part II. and the Staff Manual respectively. Title Pages will be prepared in manuscript.

Place	Date	Hour	Summary of Events and Information	Remarks and references to Appendices
MERICOURT L'ABBE	1/11/15		14 cases to CCS including 5 wounded 7 to Div Rest.	
"	2/11/15		15 cases to CCS including 10 wounded 11 to Div Rest	
"	3/11/15		2 officers sick CCS. 9 other ranks including 7 wounded 9 to Div Rest	
"	4/11/15		Cpt BRADISH RAMC 557 Amb admitted M.D. returned to duty and officer sick CCS. 6 other ranks wounded 2 wounded 20 to D.R. 10 Officer CCS sick other ranks 19 to Div Rest	
"	5/11/15			
"	6/11/15		7 cases to CCS including 2 wounded 24 to Div Rest	
"	7/11/15		Paid 40/- Found for wood cutting 7/- 6 to CCS including 1 wounded 18 to Div Rest. Orders from ADMS to hand over to 56 7A and take over 18th Divisional Rest between 10th & 13th instant. Necessary orders issued.	
"	8/11/15		11 cases to CCS including 10 wounded 14 to Div Rest. Capt. R.H. SUTHERLAND RAMC proceeded to FLIXECOURT on permanent duty on a church establishment	
"	9/11/15		Capt BRADISH to duty (557th Amb) Two officers sick 1 CCS remaining 7 other ranks to CCS including 3 wounded -13 to Div Rest. A.D.S. BRAY handed over to 56 7A and officer remaining to duty. 2 officers sick to CCS. 6 other ranks including 2 wounded to CCS	
"	10/11/15		14 to Div Rest. Advance dressing station MEAULTE handed over to 557A. Advance party to take over 18th Divisional rest	
"	11/11/15		one officer sick to Div Rest. 4 cases to CCS. 16 to D.R. 0/40 Proceeded purchase and	
"	12/11/15		5 to CCS including 3 wounded 10 to Div Rest arrived and took over Divisional Rest station. report of arrival rendered D-ADMS	
DAOURS.	13/11/15		Administration 557A M.D. wounded Rest remained 8/3 to CCS 4 to duty 9.	
"	14/11/15	1.30pm	one offr transferred from 557AB CCS. 5 cases from Div Rest to CCS. 4 duty 5	

Army Form C. 2118

WAR DIARY
or
INTELLIGENCE SUMMARY

557 A   Vol 5

M. Winder

(Erase heading not required.)

Place	Date	Hour	Summary of Events and Information	Remarks and references to Appendices
DAOURS	15-11-15		557.A. 1 to Div Rmt 2 remaining. 18th Div Rmt 5 to ees. 15 to duty remaining 77	
"	16-11-15		557.A. 1 to Dmt 1 ees 2 remaining. 18th Div Rmt 4 to ees 4 to duty remaining 79 Pte W. Smith for Lenwark	
"	17-11-15		557 A. 1 to ees 3 remaining. 18th Div Rmt 2 to ees 10 to duty remaining 78	
"	18-11-15		557 A. 2 to ees 4 to Div Rmt 3 remaining. 18th Div Rmt 2 to ees. 11 to duty remaining 84	
"	19-11-15		557 A 1 to ees 3 to Div Rmt 3 remaining. 18th Div Rmt 3 to ees. 14 to duty remaining 87	
"	20-11-15		7 A 4 men remaining 18th Div Rmt 2 to ees 7 to duty remaining 97	
"	21-11-15		7A 1 to ees 3 to Div Rmt nil remaining. 18th Div Rmt 8 to duty remaining 103	
"	22-11-15		7 A 1 ear remaining. 18 Div Rmt 5 to ees 15 to duty 105 remaining	
"	23-11-15		7.A. 18 Div Rmt 18th Div Rmt 6 to ees 10 to duty 107 remaining 1 officer admitted	
"	24-11-15		7 A. 18 Div Rmt remaining 1. - Div Rmt 5 to ees 8 to duty 110 remaining + 1 officer	
"	25-11-15		7 A. 18 Div Rmt remaining nil - Div Rmt 11 to ees. 10 to duty 109 remaining + 2 officers	
"	26-11-15		7 A. Div Rmt 1 officer 60 heads to ees 1 officer 12 other ranks to duty 10 officers 105 remaining. W 5/5 32 Pte SPRATT S. 557A Pte Rouse + hufs Z 07 4/60 Pte ELINCH J.A.S.E.M.T. 557 A killed + 2 W BARNETT A.S.E.MT 557 A wounded by enemy aeroplane at MERICOURT	
"	27-11-15		7.A. 1 officer to ees - Div Rmt 1 officer 3 Other ranks to ees. 16 to duty 97 remaining Paid 2 francs for 12 beads of chalets. Two men shown 26th buried MERICOURT today	
"	28-11-15		7.A. nil. NBJ Div Rmt 1 to ees 4 to duty 109 remaining	
"	29-11-15		7.A. 2 remaining. 18th Div Rmt 2 to ees 12 to duty 102 remaining Paid 62.60 Reichsgulden to refrain francs for new ward paid 17 3 for 2 barrels for baths	
"	30-11-15		7A. 2 to Div Rmt 2 remaining. Div Rmt 4 to ees. 12 to duty 99 remaining	

Dec 1915

18th/Xll
―――
F 155/1

55-2.a.
rst:

101
―――
7896

WAR DIARY
or
INTELLIGENCE SUMMARY

(Erase heading not required.)

Army Form C. 2118

Vol 6
M/Winder

55 Fd Amb

Place	Date	Hour	Summary of Events and Information	Remarks and references to Appendices
DAOURS	1.12.15		7.A. 1 to Div Rest 2 remain = 18th Div Rest 6 to ees. 20 to duty 89 remain.	Appx Appx
"	2.12.15		7.A. 1 to ees. 1 to Div Rest 1 to duty 2 remain. — Div Rest 5 to ees 8 to duty 99 remain Colt W.G. GORDON R.A.M.C. T.S. reported pr du[t] 1.12.15. Complete establishment of officers constitution	Appx
"	3.12.15		2A/officers Vanieillate Highland ees. 1 other rank to ees. remain 3. — 18th Div Rest 4 to ees 1 to duty remain 113. St T.A. WATSON 55 T.A. struck of strength from 2.12.15 transfer to general hosp probably time	Appx
"	4.12.15		7.A. 1 to ees. 2 to duty, 1 remain. — 18th Div Rest 5 to ees. 13 to duty 126 remain Saw C R.E. and A. in accordance with instructions to A.D.M.S. to batt. 500 yd. commencing 11th A check with adjt R.E. for necessary fatigue arrangement	Appx
"	5.12.15		Rd 2 Ph. 20 loads clinkers. 1.120 Fr Bath for had wagon. 3.25 mid fr / partitions	Appx
"	6.12.15		7.A. 1 to Div Rest. — 18th Div Rest 4 to ees. — 18th Div Rest 4 to duty remain 139	Appx
"	7.12.15		7.A. 1 to ees, 1 to duty. — 18th Div Rest 3 to ees 28 to duty remain 154 Fd 144 fr partitions Bowels	Appx
"	8.12.15		7.A. 1 remain — 18th Div Rest 4 to ees 21 to duty remain 151	Appx
"	"		7.A. 1 to ees — 18th Div Rest 1 officer to ees 4 other ranks 32 to duty remain 136 Lord Nichaan Richmond 43.00 Fr Sham Bros 137.75 Fr tunnels of dried level 2.10 Fr to put up wires & bolera for hot water for bath. R.E. unable to supply	Appx
"	9.12.15		7.A. adj — 18th Div Rest 6 to ees — 19 to duty — remain 128	Appx
"	10.12.15		7.A. 25 Div Rest 2 remain — 18th Div Rest 3 to ees 19 to duty 122 remain Ad 6.95 Fr /m 3 pit men fr summer loving clothes	Appx
"	11.12.15		7.A. 2 to Div Rest 3 remain — 18th Div Rest 5 to ees 24 to duty 114 remain	Appx
"	12.12.15		Rehn for burgade started this morning. — 7.A. 2 to Div Rest 1 to duty — 18th Div Rest 1 to ees 27 to duty 110 remain	Appx
"	13.12.15		1 officer to ees 15 to duty remain 111. Battled 385 men	Appx

WAR DIARY or INTELLIGENCE SUMMARY

Army Form C. 2118

557 M. Ewl.

Vol 6

Place	Date	Hour	Summary of Events and Information	Remarks and references to Appendices
DAOURS	14.12.15		7.A. 4 remain — 18th Div Ret 3 to ees. 20 to duty remaining 100. Batted 355 Ad 1125h for Linenwork	
"	15.12.15		7.A. 1 to ees. 2 BDR 2 nez arm — 18th in Ret 1 to ees. 11 to duty 110 remain. Capt R.H. SUTHERLAND RAMC T.E. arrived 14.11 for temporary duty	
"	16.12.15		7.A. 1 to ees. 3 BDR 1 to duty — 18th Div Ret 3 to ees. 12 to duty 126 remain	
"	17.12.15		7.A. 1 to ees 1 remain — 18th Div Ret 2 to ees 17 to duty 135 remain wounded 349.	
"	18.12.15		7.A. 2 BDR 1 to duty 2 remain — 18th Div Ret 2 to ees. 26 to duty 126 remain. Capt R.H. SUTHERLAND RAMC T.E. struck off strength, on proceeding to 5th Div (ADMS instructions)	
"	19.12.15		7.A. 1 BDR. 1 to duty — 18th Div Ret 2 to ees. 6 to duty 153 remain. Batted 393	
"	20.12.15		7.A. 18th Div Ret 2 to ees. 10 to duty 167 remain. S.M. TURNER appointed temp Qu ar. RAME from 15.12.15 & posted an acum to 557 A. field authority (118,965/1 (A.M.D.) application submitted 30th Nov. Recommended that along with S.S.t SHELTON be promoted S.M. to complete war establishment 53 h/nds in Lnt in neighbouring villages Batted 235	
"	21.12.15		7.A. 1 remain — 18th Div Ret 4 to ees. 23 to duty 156 remain. Batted 343	
"	22.12.15 23.12.15		7.A. 1 to Div Lent. 2 remain — 18th Div Ret 2 to ees. 16 to duty 159 remain. Batted 484	
"	"		7.A. 7 to Div Ret 1 remain — 18th Div Ret 1 to ees 32 to duty 168 remain. Batted 500	
"	24.12.15		7.A. 2 to ees. 1 BDR — 18th Div Ret 4 to ees 20 to duty 176 remain. Pd 60 /p drowning /pfe 180 Bales for wagon 1125h Limbeworth	
"	25.12.15		7.A. 2 to ees. 1 remain — 18th Div Ret 4 to ees. 18 to duty 184 remain	
"	26.12.15		7.A. 15 Div Ret 3 remain — 18th Div Ret 5 to ees 27 to duty 169 remain. Batted 552	
"	27.12.15		7.A. 3 to ees @ 250 y Ret 4 remain — 18th Div Let 3 to ees 50 to duty 135 remain. wounded 184	
"	28.12.15		7.A. 1 to ees 6 Div Let 6 remain — 18th Div Ret 4 to ees 15 to duty 142 remain	

Army Form C. 2118

Vol 6
M Winder

WAR DIARY
or
INTELLIGENCE SUMMARY

557d Amb

(Erase heading not required.)

Place	Date	Hour	Summary of Events and Information	Remarks and references to Appendices
DAOURS	29.12.15		7A. 1 to C.C.S. 3 to Div Rest 1 remaining — 18th Div Rest 20 to duty 138 remain	appx
"	30.12.15		7A. 15 to CCS 1 to duty 2 remain — 18th Div Rest 9 to CCS 14 to duty 139 remain Capt W.G. GORDON detached for temporary duty with 7th Redoubt	appx
"	31.12.15		7A. 2 to Div Rest 3 remain — 18th Div Rest 5 to CCS 13 to duty 144 remain	appx

55th F.A.
Vol: 7

18th Div
F/155/2

Jan 1916

WAR DIARY
or
INTELLIGENCE SUMMARY

Army Form C. 2118

(Erase heading not required.)

557 Ambulance Vol 7

Place	Date	Hour	Summary of Events and Information	Remarks and references to Appendices
DAOURS	1.1.16		F.A. 1 to C.C.S. 2 to Div Rest. Remain — 18th Div Rest 1 to C.C.S. 24 to duty 145 remain	
	2.1.16		F.A.R. 1 to Div Rest — 18th Div Rest 2 to C.C.S. 24 to duty 139 remain	
	3.1.16		F.A. nil — 18th Div Rest 3 to C.C.S. 18 to duty 143 remain	
	4.1.16		F.A. 1 to C.C.S. 2 remain — 18th Div Rest 3 to C.C.S. 11 to duty 138 remain	
	5.1.16		F.A. 2 to Div Rest — 18th Div Rest 1 to C.C.S. 18 to duty 139 remain	
	6.1.16		F.A. nil — 18th Div Rest 5 to C.C.S. 28 to duty 134 remain	
	7.1.16		F.A. 1 remaining — 18 Div Rest 2 to C.C.S. 26 to duty 129 remaining	
	8.1.16		F.A. 1/6 CCS 1 to duty — 18 Div Rest 2, 6 CCS 24 to duty 121 remaining. Lt J.W. TURNER RAMC T.C. admitted	
	9.1.16		F.A. 2 remaining — 18 Div: Rest 3 6 CCS 26 to duty 103 remaining. Lt J.W.TURNER RAMC T.C. admitted	
	10.1.16		F.A. 1 Div: rsh. 16 July 2 remaining — 18th Div: Rest 3 6 CCS 7 to duty 109 remaining. BRAY	
	11.1.16		F.A. 2 remaining — 18 Div: Rest 2 6 CCS 1 to duty 117 remaining. BRAYVILLE early/duty rel'd	
	12.1.16		F.A. nil - 18 Div Rel' 1 6 CCS 17 to duty 114 remaining. F.A. headquarters posted GMERICOURT	
MERICOURT L'ABBE	13.1.16		Visited A.D.S. BRAY and VILLE, found all correct.	
	14.1.16		Paid a visit from line. trouble was killed	
	15.1.16		Visited A.D.S. BRAY & VILLE all correct	
	16.1.16		Visited VILLE Bath. LT. E.McINTYRE & J. HUMPHREYS RAME T.C.	
	17.1.16		Visited BRAY A.D.S.	
	18.1.16		Visited VILLE	
	19.1.16			
	20.1.16		Visited BRAY	
	21.1.16		Lt HUMPHREYS to 4th Division, struck off strength. Lt HWS WRIGHT RAMC T.C. joined from 54 F.A.	
	22.1.16		Visited BRAY. Started T.A.B. inoculation. Al 74.0 O. for hospital ward Rome VILLE	
	23.1.16			
	24.1.16			

WAR DIARY
or
INTELLIGENCE SUMMARY
(Erase heading not required.)

Army Form C. 2118

Vol 7

557 A

Place	Date	Hour	Summary of Events and Information	Remarks and references to Appendices
	25.1.16		Visited VILLE	
	26.1.16		"	
	27.1.16		Visited VILLE new engine now arrived	
	28.1.16		" RE expect to have it working in 14 days	
	29.1.16		Butted 3496 at V'ille for week ending 29th inclusive	
	30.1.16		Paid 11.25 to M. Lenne	
	31.1.16		Visited VILLE.	

5 S. F.A.
18th Div
Vol. 8.

Feb 1916

Army Form C. 2118

WAR DIARY
or
INTELLIGENCE SUMMARY
(Erase heading not required.)

Vol 8.
M/Winter

55 7.A.

Place	Date	Hour	Summary of Events and Information	Remarks and references to Appendices
MERICOURT L'ABBE	1.2.16		Visited BRAY. 2 Field Ambulance of 7th Division sent advance party to take over this A.D.S.	Appx
"	2.2.16		Orders received for move of Hq 7.A. to PONT. NOYELLES.	Appx
"	3.2.16		Advance dressing station party from BRAY rejoined - posted to VILLE le beuve division.	notes contd
"	4.2.16		Advance party. 1 officer + 6 O.R. to PONT NOYELLES.	
"	5.2.16		Headquarters hauled over billets & moved to new area. 11.0 am	
PONT. NOYELLES	"	2.0 pm	Headquarters arrived. Present distribution 55 7.A. Lens Down division at PONT. NOYELLES. Beaver division at VILLE betta. Strength Headquarters 104 including officers. Report of move to A.D.M.S.	Appx
"	6.2.16		Fatigues manned everywhere office a conference cleaned. Fodder lorry with 2 Thed disinfector started from 30th Division now working for infantry attached.	Appx notes contd
"	7.2.16		Fodder lorry in use by R.W. Kent.	
"	8.2.16		Received at glover baths to be kept handing allotment arrangements for detail	
"	9.2.16		Visited VILLE. Petrol engine now working, mechanical washer working, a large amount of dirty washing remains to be done. 7th Division been worked in addition to our division.	Appx
"	10.2.16		Paid 11.25 pt for lines for orderlies	
"	11.2.16		Took over quite a lot to open up accommodation for 40 patient, with A.D.M.S. School nearby.	Appx notes
"	12.2.16		notified 54 7.A. patient can be received. Seven local sick.	Appx
"	13.2.16		18 cases transferred from 54 7.A. Lieut W.g. GORDON RAMC to No S.C.S. for duty.	
"	14.2.16		23 remaining 1 to duty 22 remained. Cat't R.T.C. ROBERTSON RAMC S.R. joined for duty from Hq 5 C.E.S.	
"	15.2.16		9 came from 54 7.A. 31 remain. # PL W. WILLIAMS RAMC to 7 RW Kents as M.O. and strength of ambulance staff	
"	16.2.16		No 53788 Pte WINGROVE. 39571 Pte MORLEY. 9. 38791 Pte THORNTON m recommended for C.M. staff of no duty + further from Stonehouse went in use a dressing station. Patients stolen belonging to shoemaker	Appx
			[illegible] 5 canvas.	

WAR DIARY or INTELLIGENCE SUMMARY

Army Form C. 2118
Vol 8
557A

Place	Date	Hour	Summary of Events and Information	Remarks and references to Appendices
PONT. NOYELLES	17.2.16		Foden lorry left for RIBEMONT. 1 ear to e.c.s. 6 to duty 39 remain	Appx
"	18.2.16		7.g.e.M. on leave noted 16th. 2 men to e.c.s. 4 to duty 40 remain	Appx
"	19.2.16		3 to duty 39 cases remain	Appx
"	20.2.16		2 to e.c.s. 8 to duty 29 remain	Appx
"	21.2.16		1 to duty 39 remain. Appointed President of a 7.g.e.M. h/CRA 18th division. referred order for ruling under K.R. & M.M.L. rule in[illegible] fresh president appointed	Appx
"	22.2.16		2 to e.c.s. 10 to duty 27 remain. Proceeding of 7.g.e.M. of 1st cut on error noted 16th int hand./std 28 days 7.S.P. No 1 in each case confirmed by Maj. Gen. F.I. MAXSE 21st int	Appx
"			Capt C.W. TREHERNE R.A.M.C. 557A admitted 23rd hysenia. OR 2 to duty 26 remain	Appx
"	23.2.16		LT WRIGHT H.W.S. to 84th Brigade R.7A as h/o on 21st int. a struck off ambulance accordingly. Capt YATES. g.o. from 84 Brigade R7A and [illegible] strength 21st int [illegible]	Appx
			1 officer sick. Transferred to W.Rest. 4 men to e.c.s. 3 to duty 26 remain	Appx
"	24.2.16		Capt TREHERNE taken off sick list. 2 men to duty 22 remain	Appx
"	25.2.16			Appx
"	26.2.16		1 to e.c.s. 6 to duty 18 remain	Appx
"	27.2.16		1 to e.c.s. 5 to duty 13 remain	Appx
"	28.2.16		3 to duty 13 remain	Appx
"	29.2.16		1 officer sick (accidental wound) to air List. 1 man to e.c.s. 4 to duty 9 remain	Appx

55 J Amb
Vol 9410

1st Div

March 1916
April 1916

Army Form C. 2118

Vol 9

WAR DIARY
or
INTELLIGENCE SUMMARY

55 F.A.

(Erase heading not required.)

Place	Date	Hour	Summary of Events and Information	Remarks and references to Appendices
PONT. NOYELLES	1.3.16		1 to duty. 11 remain. Visited Batt. VILLE	
"	2.3.16		3 to duty. 13 remain.	
"	3.3.16		5 to duty. 11 remain.	
"	4.3.16		1 to ees. 10 remain. Orders from ADMS to take over chateau at CORBIE from 22 F.A. Report move to be completed by 7th inst. 7 F.A. headquarters will move to 6th Bevas division from VILLE	
" CORBIE	5.3.16		7, 5 to 18th Div in rest. 5 to duty. Towards closed	
	6.3.16		Headquarters arrived and took over chateau from 22 F.A. Report to ADMS. Took over from 22 F.A. 30 cases shifted of 18th division	
"	7.3.16		4 transfer. 34 remain. Bevas division opened headquarters. Both and lumber at VILLE handed over to 7th & 18th Div sanitary section respectively.	
"	8.3.16		1 to ees. 1 to 7th Div in rest 3 to duty. 31 remain.	
"	9.3.16		5 to C.E.S. 42 remain. Visited BRAY, BRON FAY collecting post & R.A.P. CARNOY with D.A.D.M.S.	
"	10.3.16		6 to ees. 7 to duty 40 remain. No 3/521 P&FLEET collecting post under re-construction from 4.12.15	
"	11.3.16		2 to ees. 4 to duty 41 remain. Visited SUZANNE & MARICOURT R.A.P. (4) with P.A.D.M.S.	
"	12.3.16		6 to ees 2 to duty 43 remain. Capt. WTREHERNE R.A.M.C. SR. stand off. transferred 11th to 3rd army	
"	13.3.16		3 to ees 4 to duty 48 remain.	
"	14.3.16		3 to ees, 1 being made from 7th R.W. survey met to ees 5 to duty 54 remain. Inspection by ADMS 4th army & DDMS 13th corps. Operation orders ADMS ambulance to move to new ADS. BRAY from 96th dated 17th main dressing station CHIPILLY to be completed by noon 20th inst	
"	15.3.16		6 to ees 11 to duty 43 remain. Visited CHIPILLY & BRAY to arrange to take over there main station from 30th F. amb.	

… Army Form C. 2118

WAR DIARY
INTELLIGENCE SUMMARY
(Erase heading not required.) AMIENS sheet 17 55 7 A

Vol 9
W. Wünsche

Place	Date	Hour	Summary of Events and Information	Remarks and references to Appendices
CORBIE	16.3.16		9 t cc s 10 to duty 42 remain	
"	17.3.16		O/C T.H.CONNOLLY RAMC T.C. reported for duty & taking up strength 7th 2 in. offr Rest stn — 59 remain	
"	18.3.16		A.D.S. BRAY completed. 5 evacuations t cc s including 1 measles 7 N.W Kutz (sent to H.e.c.s 9 to duty 53 remain. Advance party to take over main dressing station sent to CHIPILLY	
"	19.3.16		One officer admitted to 2½ sta transferred to 21 gen Rest. 2 evacuations t cc s 17 to Div Rest (7A) 17 to duty remain 23 transferred to 96 T.A at 12 noon. Cpt CONNOLLY RAMC T.C. RDA qu attd. off Report to A.D.M.S.	
"	20.3.16		Took over main dressing station from 96 TA. Taken over 128. cases from 96 TA	
CHIPILLY	"	12 noon	Ambulance in position as follows — Collecting Post BRONFAY FARM? 1 officer 14 men. 6 wheels from 54 F.A. " " MARICOURT WOOD men 2 wheels " " SUZANNE 1 officer 14 men 1 N.C.O Brown 3 wheels 1 2 wheeler R.A.M.C All convoys in A.D.S. BRAY 3 officers 42 other ranks RAMC. with 3 tent sections and one horse Ambulance wagon. main dressing station has attached 6 bearer under an officer in charge from 4th army with 2 officers + 20 men attached from 56 FA This is a portion of main dressing station	

WAR DIARY or INTELLIGENCE SUMMARY

Army Form C. 2118

Vol 9

AMIENS Sheet 17; 57A

Place	Date	Hour	Summary of Events and Information	Remarks and references to Appendices
CHIPILLY	21.3.16		admitted 36 including 8 wounded 13 to CCS 15 to DR Died 2. admitted 3 officers 1 to CCS 2 remain 130 remain	
"	22.3.16		admitted 2 officers transferred 4 to Base not admitted OR 27 including 15 wounded 18 to CCS 22 to DR 10 4 remain 1 death from GAS SPRAY deed. Visited SUZANNE & MARICOURT with A.D.M.S. went over ground to find alternative line of evacuation from CARNOY. R.G.E.M. on 31521 Pte FLEET. Demetrin in event from 13.2.16 admitted 2 officers & transferred to CCS 305 21 to CCS 3 to duty remain 126	
"	23.3.16		" OR 16 including 6 wounded	
"	24.3.16		admitted 20 1 to CCS 11 to dut 134 remain	
"	25.3.16		1 officer admitted attempted to reach to [?] Rest 10 evacuees including 4 wounded ((2&9)) 2 to DR died 1 17 to dut, Visited SUZANNE & VAUX. Visited SUZANNE & V.C. rector 2 officers admitted 1 to CCS 1 to DR	
"	26.3.16		27 OR 3 OR CCS including 1 wounded 15 to DR 9 to dut 144 remain	
"	27.3.16		2 officers admitted 75 OR CCS. 2 to DR 14 to dut 156 remain 35 O.R. admitted 4 admitted including 3 (T & OS) wounded 3 remain	
"	28.3.16		2 officers removed OR 56 admitted included 19 wounded 24 to CCS 18 to dut 170 remain	
"	29.3.16		Visited BRONFAY Form 3 officers admitted (1 transferred to HCCS) 5 remain	
"	30.3.16		OR 24 admitted 11 to CCS 15 to 18 DR 14 to duty remain 154 Capt # F.J. L. BRADISH struck off strength of unit and posted to sand di to Command 92 7A Admitted 2 officers 1 wounded 12 to CCS 2 1 to DR 15 to duty 137 remain	
"	31.3.16		officer 1 admitted & remain OR 38 admitted 7 to CCS 8 to DR 11 to dut 14 remain Visited SUZANNE & MARICOURT	

WAR DIARY or INTELLIGENCE SUMMARY

Army Form C. 2118

55 7.A. Vol ? (?)

Place	Date	Hour	Summary of Events and Information	Remarks and references to Appendices
CHIPILLY	1.4.16		admitted 3 officers 1 to ees 10 remain (includes Capt RICHARDS 55 7A Pyrexia) O.R. admitted 39 including 12 wounded 17 to ees 6 to D.R. 20 to duty. 145 remain	
"	2.4.16		admitted 35 including 7 wounded 10 to ees, 9 to D.R. 13 to duty 148 remain. 10 officers remain	
"	3.4.16		admitted 1 officer remain 11. O.R. 34 admitted 32. O.R. 11 to ees. 8 to D.R. 1 died. 16 to duty 145 remain	
"	4.4.16		Capt M.H. LISTER R.A.M.C. T.E. Wanted for duty on evacuation of 3rd. officer 1 admitted 1 to 7th D.F. Rest officers 11 remain. Visited SUZANNE & R.A.P. Y3. O.R. 34 admitted including 8 wounded 9 to ees 7 to D.R. 14 to duty 149 remain. Capt RICHARDS 55 7A to duty. 10 officers remain	
"	5.4.16		O.R. admitted 32 including 2 wounded 8 to ees 11 to D.R. 17 to duty 145 remain 1 officer admitted 11 remain	
"	6.4.16		O.R. admitted 35 including 6 wounded 9 to ees 21 to D.R. 9 to duty 141 remain	
"	7.4.16		4 officers admitted 8 to duty 12 remain. O.R. 32 admitted including 5 wounded 5 to ees 5 to D.R. 12 to duty 151 remain	
"	8.4.16		12 officers remain. O.R. 34 admitted including 8 wounded 9 to D.R. 11 to ees 21 to duty 144 remain. Visited A.D.S./BRAY	
"	9.4.16		1 officer to ees 12 remain. 26 O.R. admitted including 1 wound 8 to ees 12 to duty 150 remain	
"	10.4.16		1 officer admitted 13 remain. 26 O.R. including 3 wounded 12 to ees 13 to D.R. 6 to duty 145 remain. Visited CARNOY with ADMS	
"	11.4.16		officers 3 admitted including 2 wounded 2 to ees 2 to duty remain 12. O.R. 42 admitted including 3 wounds 11 to ees 3 to D.R. 18 to duty 153 remain. Lt. W.A.L. MARRIOTT RAMC T.P. joined 11th Reinforcement	
"	12.4.16		Officer 10 remain 15 to duty 1 to ees 11 remain. O.R. 31 admitted including 5 wounded 13 to ees 14 to D.R. 1 died 14 to duty 145 remain	

WAR DIARY or INTELLIGENCE SUMMARY

Army Form C. 2118
Vol 10

Place	Date	Hour	Summary of Events and Information	Remarks and references to Appendices
CHIPILLY	13.4.16		Admitted 1 officer 2 to duty 10 remain. 35 admn OR. 6 to duty incld 11 wounded. 1 officer admitted 6 to CCS 13 to DR. 16 to duty 143 remain	
"	14.4.16		OR. 62 admns including 36 wounded 45 to CCS 8 to DR. 13 to duty 145 remain. CCS convs include 5 to HEEC, Juma nearer. Visited CARNOY with ADMS 13th – Midday 13th reported to me that about 26 seriously wounded were at CARNOY detailed 9 op. nads with stretchers & blankets to reinforce BRONFAY e.p. & the while to weed & evacuate these cases by trench during daylight. Capt HARTGILL in charge. There were 15 cases. & the Regtl M.O. stated they were all unfit for removal. Apparently not knowing knowledge of removal by trenches, with much difficulty his objections were overcome with regard to some cases who were brought down AD to have permanent to complete evacuation at dusk. Wish were received at ADs. were stated to have the wounds stinking. The evacuation from this front in a very long trained convoy, but I can early be home. the cases when received at A.D.S. were stated to have the wounds stinking –	
	15.4.16		Officers 2 admitted 1 discharged to remain. OR. 19 admitted including 2 wounded 6 to CCS 6 to DR. 1 died 17 to duty 134 remain	
"	16.4.16		Officers 2 to CCS. 10 remain. OR. 38 admns includg 6 wounded 15 to CCS 14 to DR. 8 to duty remain 135. Visited BRONFAY & CARNOY	
"	17.4.16		Officers 1 admitted 1 to duty. 10 remain. OR. 27 admitted including 8 wounded 10 to CCS 5 to DR. Died 1. 22 to duty 124 remain	
"	18.4.16		Officers 5 admitted 3 to CCS 1 to duty 11 remain	
	19.4.16		OR. 31 admns including 4 wounded 10 to CCS 4 to DR. 11 to duty 130 remain. Officers 2 to duty 10 to R.S. 9 remain. 1 wounded 6 to CCS 11 to DR. 9 to duty 130 remain	

Army Form C. 2118

Vol 10
M Winslee

55 F.A.

WAR DIARY
or
INTELLIGENCE SUMMARY
(Erase heading not required.)

Instructions regarding War Diaries and Intelligence Summaries are contained in F.S. Regs., Part II. and the Staff Manual respectively. Title Pages will be prepared in manuscript.

Place	Date	Hour	Summary of Events and Information	Remarks and references to Appendices
CHIPILLY	20.4.16	—	Remain 9 officers O.R. 47 admissions including 14 wounded 16 to duty but 13 to duty 136 remain	[sig]
"	21.4.16		admitted 1 officer 1 to duty 9 remain O.R. 31 admitted including 6 wounded 14 to ees 6 to DR 18 to duty 129 remain	[sig]
"	22.4.16		officer 1 admission 2 to ees & remain O.R. 34 admissions including 7 wounded 10 to ees 5 to DR 17 to duty 131 remain	[sig]
"	23.4.16		officer 1 admission 4 to ees 8 remain O.R. 32 admissions including 4 wounded 10 to ees. 12 to DR 2 died 16 to duty 123 remain	[sig]
"	24.4.16		officer 2 admissions 2 to ees 8 remain O.R. 28 admissions including 7 wounded 8 to ees 11 to DR. 10 died 17 to DR 115 remain into BRONFAY.	[sig]
"	25.4.16		officer 3 admissions 4 to ees 2 to duty 8 remain O.R. 43 admitted including 11 wounded 16 to ees 9 to DR 1 died 9 to duty 123 remain	[sig]
"	26.4.16		officer admitted 3 included 2 wounded 5 to ees 8 remain O.R. 41 admissions included 10 wounded 14 to ees 7 to DR 1 died 7 to duty 135 remain	[sig]
"	27.4.16		Visited BERTANGLES et PICQUIGNY to arrange moves with 7A., returning admitted 2 officers 2 to ees 8 remain O.R. 46 admissions 7 to ees 23 to DR. 1 died 12 to duty 138 remain	[sig]
"	28.4.16		admitted 1 officer wounded 1 to ees 8 remain O.R. 66 admitted including 42 wounded 4 to ees 19 to DR 2 died 15 to duty 126 remain	[sig]
"	29.4.16		officer 1 admission 7 to duty 2 remain O.R. 41 admission including 5 wounded 12 to ees 18 to DR 1 died 16 to duty 120 remain	[sig]
"	30.4.16		[faded text] ... 1 to CCS 11 to Amb ... military 20 wounded, 14 to CCS, 12 DRS, 1 died, 16 to duty, remaining 112	[sig]

1875 Wt. W393/826 1,000,000 4/15 J.B.C. & A. A.D.S.S./Forms/C. 2118.

No. 55 F. Amb.

18th D25

May 1916.

COMMITTEE FOR THE
MEDICAL HISTORY OF THE WAR
Date 26 JUN. 1916

WAR DIARY
or
INTELLIGENCE SUMMARY
(Erase heading not required.)

Army Form C. 2118

Vol 11

M J Manly
3/3 J Amb

Place	Date	Hour	Summary of Events and Information	Remarks and references to Appendices
Chipilly	1-5-16		Anneux. 2 Officers missing. 1 wounded. 1 evacuated to CCS. 2 officers. 1 officer sick, and 3 remaining. After Rouke H.Q admitted initially 15 wounded. 14 evacuated and 1 sick to CCS. 14 O.R. on sick list. 17 O.R. to duty and 7 O.M. R.C.O. and 3 men proceed to BERTANGLES. and remaining 102.	near
"	2.5.16.		Admitted 3 Officers, remaining Co. O.R. admitted 36 including 5 wounded. 5 evacuated. One officer and 3. O.R. proceeded to BERTANGLES.	near
"	3-5-16.		Admitted no officer. 2 to duty. 5 to duty. 5 transferred to 98 F? Amb. remaining fell. O.R. 52 admitted including 6 wounded. Sup to C.C.S. 1 to duty. 1 to 96 F? Amb.; 1 to 98 F? Amb. Remaining 102.	near
Lahoussoye	4-5-16		Hospital closed and books closed 12 noon. One officer and 95 O.R. proceeded to frontline camp.	near
Bertangles	5-5-16		Field Ambulance arrived 11.30 a.m.	near
"	6.5.16.		One case taken to 54 F? Amb appeasing.	near
"	7-5-16		Three cases taken to 54 F? Amb at Picquigny.	near
"	8.5.16		No cases to CCS.	near
"	9.5.16.		5 cases sent to 54 F? 7? Amb.	near
"	10-5-16		1 case sent to 54 F? Amb.	near
"	11-5-16		3 cases sent to 54 F? Amb.	near
"	12.5.16.		6 cases sent to 54 F? 7? Amb.	near
"	13-5-16.		4 cases sent to 54 F? 2? Amb.	near
"	14-5-16		4 cases sent to 54 F? 7? Amb.	near
"	15-5-16		5 cases sent to 54 F? Picquigny.	near
"	16.5.16		4 cases sent to 54 F? 7? Amb.	near
"	17.5.16		The last batch of 5 to 54 F? Amb.	near
"	18.5.16.		4 cases sent to 54 F? 7? Amb. Capt No 15231 Cpl MILLARD proceeding from BERTANGLES to PICIQUIGNY met with an accident with patients	near
"	19.5.16		10 cases sent to 54 F? 7? Amb.	near
"	20.5.16		15 cases sent to 54 F? 7? Amb. a 5. N.C.O. and men appointed to 4 SCCS for temporary duty	near
"	23.5.16		Court of Enquiry on damage to Cas 15231 damaged 19.5.16	

1875 Wt. W593/826 1,000,000 4/15 J.B.C. & A. A.D.S.S./Forms/C. 2118.

WAR DIARY
or
INTELLIGENCE SUMMARY

Army Form C. 2118

Vol II
557A

Place	Date	Hour	Summary of Events and Information	Remarks and references to Appendices
BERTANGLES	24.5.16		Rain	
"	25.5.16		motor cycle damaged by shed falling in, cycle sent in to D.S.E.	
"	26.5.16		M.T. establishment reduced by 1 motor cycle & 1 cpl. G.H.Q. authority cycle & cpl handed in	
"	27.5.16		orders received re baggage & stores in excess to scale, to be dumped when ordered	
"	28.6.16		in case of an advance. Vacancy staff taken to empty with orders re stores etc — in case of our advance	
"	29.5.16		LT. J.R. ELWOOD R.A.M.C. T.C. reported for duty last night A/Capt RT.E. ROBERTSON R.A.M.C. S.R. to 39 C.C.S. & truck off attempt this a.m.	
"	31.5.16		Went to ETINEHEM. with A.D.M.S.	

No. 55 7A.

June 1916.

COMMITTEE FOR THE
MEDICAL HISTORY OF THE WAR
Date 5 AUG. 1916

Vol 12
Army Form C. 2118

WAR DIARY
or
INTELLIGENCE SUMMARY
(Erase heading not required.)

557A Vol 12

M Winch had the ALBERT
[signed initials]

Place	Date	Hour	Summary of Events and Information	Remarks and references to Appendices
BERTANGLES	1.6.16		Conference at ADMS office with RMO's 55 Div [pajto] sent AE. PRIEZ RAME TE. [mfrsell] for duty with amb & taken on, temp.	
"	3.6.16		Visited BRAY & CARNOY to inspect car progress of medical arrangements near Carnoy to report on new arrangements to ADMS.	
"	5.6.16			
"	9.6.16			
"	10.6.16		SAPPER Corner (L 10 & 11. Map Albert's.)	
			1. Two of dug outs are 6'.6" in width, require 8' so that there dug outs can be used for lying cases.	
			2. A pinch will be contain about 3 people 10 yards S of BRONFAY RD at this point, this to control road traffic. Gas protection required.	
			Not accepted by CRE.2 accepted.	
			BRONFAY	
			2 dug outs, both require gas protection, which as yet to be finished. Total accommodation 36 = 18 stretchers. Approach must be made, to enable cars to circle CRE.2. will do.	
			BRICKLANE (CARNOY)	
			Accommodation now 18 this can be increased to 30 by further huddling. Gas protection is required for windows. A house called "ship" is being made in vicinity. For the present purpose congestion and

Vol 12

WAR DIARY

INTELLIGENCE SUMMARY

Army Form C. 2118

55 7A Vol 12

Place	Date	Hour	Summary of Events and Information	Remarks and references to Appendices
BERTANGLES	10.6.16		insufficient. I see no possible means of gas protection in their air cover. Thinning out of the garrison of Shrapnel dug in the mane. Maj ALBERT evacuated sick 10/6/16. Two small dressing stations are they	
			MEREHISTON AVENUE 5 shelters = 60 cases. 36 stretchers overhead protection averages 2'6". No gas protection at all, doors or windows. I believe there sufficient dug outs for the men have been occupied making & making good dug outs for D.Hq., to the detriment of our legitimate duties. The C.R.E. informs me that the great hindrance has been material, which quite apart from this point, my note duty in the welfare of the wounded. This is not sufficiently safeguarded. I have asked the C.R.E. to put some rider on the road, any vehicle is let in may have be blocked under the minimum can be drawn aside.	
	11.6.16		Accompanied ADMS & DADMS XIII Corps to inspect above medical arrangements. 50 German slates.	

WAR DIARY or INTELLIGENCE SUMMARY

Army Form C. 2118

557A Vol 12

Place	Date	Hour	Summary of Events and Information	Remarks and references to Appendices
BERTANGLES	12.6.16		Operation orders ADMS. 10th int. F.A. to move to SAILLY LE SEC. Divis workshop parties.	
SAILLY LE SEC	13.6.16		Necessary alteration orders issued. Camp completed 5.0 pm between SAILLY & BRAY	
"	15.6.16		+ VAUX + on high ground N of same village. Activity in WELCOME WOOD midway. Visited MDS. 96 F.A. Could arrange for handing over of entire equipment. Summers bonus required. Pd. 32.95 fr for material for ad cam plays. 11.0 hrs 14th (OP) not time in to midnight.	
"	16.6.16		Operation orders from ADMS. move to GROVETOWN Camp near Bray BRAY 17th	
GROVETOWN	17.6.16		Hq at GROVETOWN 12 noon. Saw DADMS re working parties only 14 OR now with unfurnils to carry on. 60 engaged to return morning 18th. Visited BRONFAY – CARNOY.	
"	18.6.16		Issued operation orders for move into battle position arrived complete night 19/20. Hy at Sapp SAPPER house. I late attached 19 OR. 10 officers + detach at CARNOY. Capt HARTGILL in charge of medical arrangement CARNOY Reserve division Capt LISTER & 20 officers 91 OR. Advance dressing station BRICK LANE & MERCHISTON 2 rooms OR 17 + 10 two officers in each dressing station.	
BRONFAY			Hq offices 19 OR. + detach 10 OR. RAME. 20 nurseries. 10 ambulance wagon orderlies T.24 transport for ADS(R). Dugout filled with troops. advanced from CARNOY with equipment unable to move into place when dug outs were cleared. Referred to ADMS. that a am instructed to stand fast until further orders ADMS instructed to that full completed arrangement	
	19.6.16		BRONFAY collecting post completed. removing a 2 gm payment. Paid 69.60 fr, to 6 cdrville hand laundry for driving stations + 20 francs for making up 100 advance flags.	
"	20.6.16		ADS at CARNOY & BRONFAY.	
"	21.6.16		Lt N.B. SANDERS RAME T.S. joined & taken on strength.	

Army Form C. 2118

WAR DIARY
or
INTELLIGENCE SUMMARY

(Erase heading not required.)

M/Winder 55?A V of 12

ALBERT
trench sheet 1/40,000

Place	Date	Hour	Summary of Events and Information	Remarks and references to Appendices
GROVETOWN	22.6.16		LT ELWOOD tries for temporary duty. Capt P.E. CHAPMAN attached from 54?A.	
	23.6.16		Visited CARNOY, unable to get A.D.S? which have not yet been vacated by troops. Reported as under to A.D.M.S. I have to report that 9 am unable to obtain possession of the A.D.S at BRICK ALLEY & HEREHISTON AVENUE. I have rather less than 7000 lbs weight of equipment to be placed in each series of dug outs. The stores for the 2nd & newer A.D.S. have to be carried some distance. Unless I can even [?] these dug outs I shall be unable to arrange for reception of wounded. It may be impossible for me to get these stores in place during the midst of operations. As far as my information goes 9 am in no position to accept responsibility. In the success of the medical arrangement at CARNOY.	
"	24.6.16		Went to A.D.M.S. re representative by 47 new dug outs at my disposal from	
L.I.O. Q.I.I	25.6.16		25?th Artillery preparation started. Moved in to Battle stations as notified & rehearsed. 10.6.16 To the charge of arrangement for counts & evacuation XIII corps. SAPPER CORNER completed. Collection completed. BRONAY 50 stretcher cases. more troops Station in mains. handed for lying down cases. more trees BRICKALLEY dressing Station. weather, kitchen [?] BRONAY complete except in 5?th dug out HEREHISTON AVENUE. I motor by Lut BRONAY to SAPPER CORNER. 3 motor Ambulances SAPPER CORNER	
"	26.6.16		Capt MACKENZIE RAMC is reported attached in strength Horse ambulances 3 at night to MARICOURT + CARNOY. Weather improved to clear. ordered to 4?th SAPPER CORNER. Visited CARNOY now weather most historical 20 cases. Owing to lack of accommodation infantry are sheltering in the name. Two dug outs at HEREHISTON still occupied by troops on understanding they place immediately the dug outs are required.	

1875 Wt. W593/826 1,000,000 4/15 J.B.C. & A. A.D.S.S./Forms/C. 2118.

WAR DIARY
or INTELLIGENCE SUMMARY

Army Form C. 2118

557A Vol 12

Place	Date	Hour	Summary of Events and Information	Remarks and references to Appendices
L10 c.1.1.	26.6.16		ALBERT (continued shut 1/40,000) Artillery preparation increasing. Some shells in BRAY.	
"	27.6.16		Considerable number of cases from ADS. Casn learning about cases from 183 pistol to have been sent through. Visited Post BRON 7A.Y. and have ambulance shifted last night near MARICOURT. Arrangements made for teams at ready to pull it out tonight. DDMS instructed that Collecting stations for walking wounded, which has been formed by Coln at L13d should be made use of until some of shell flash sent down. Some genuine majority of wounds shrapnel, a number of shell flash sent down. Visited BRON 7AY & 30 & 3w ADS DILLON to secy. some nights newcantation. transport was satisfactory.	
"	28.6.16		Y day deflagration changed to 48 hours later before assault. Visited CARNOY. visited order 12 noon for 56 bearers to proceed to CARNOY & 54 to be relieved at GROVETOWN CAMP. 2.0 pm received order changing – moved orders to 56 & 54 to go back. 8.0 pm 56 bearers ordered to CARNOY to accordingly cancelled. Trenches very wet, a raised surface way down cases.	
"	29.6.16		had off pelting rain this morning. Quiet day not many casualties. Visited CARNOY. Beaumont SAPPER CORNER.	
"	30.6.16		Here somewhat today. Visited BRON7AY. ordered remainder of 56 7A bearer division to CARNOY. 547A Bearer Division to GROVETOWN CAMP. O.C. bearers informal warned him that all of his bearers might be ordered to move at 7.0 pm at very short notice. Authority for these moves delegated to me by ADMS 18th division. Time of further assault July 1st unknown to me.	

18/Vol 13

55th Field Amb.
July 1916

55TH
FIELD AMBULANCE

COMMITTEE FOR THE
MEDICAL HISTORY OF THE WAR
Date 31 AUG. 1916

SECRET

A.D.M.S.
18th Division

War diary for July 1916 forwarded
in accordance with 18th Div R.O. no
522 d/ 15/7/16

M J Winder
Lt Col RAMC
DC 557A

To 8th Div
forwarded

1/8/16

A J Clark
A/Lt Col
A/D.M.S. 18 Div

Collect all war diaries
for

WAR DIARY or INTELLIGENCE SUMMARY

Army Form C. 2118

55 7A Vol. 13

M/ Winter
or
Maj ALBERT
Commandant
(40,000)

Place	Date	Hour	Summary of Events and Information	Remarks and references to Appendices
L.10.c.1.1	1.7.16	6.30am	Intense artillery preparation for the	
		7.30am	Infantry Assault. Objective MONTAUBAN & North toward MAMETZ taken by 9.0am. Walking wounded arrived & entrained in large numbers, the 2 officers. Sealed ones sent to 1 B.D. walking & by horse ambulance - at least 700 included were all motors called up by 6.0 hr. 30th Division reported A.D.S. clear of all walkers & stretchers by 4.0 hr. About 150 stretcher cases initiated 30 hr. Congestion at VIELLE ARMY 4.0 hr. Constant procession of cars clearing. Then A.D.S. caught up, not so clear, 50 constant procession of cars could not proceed & later very slowly owing to the road surface being very bad. OM 547A Served up orders up by 11.0am. Bombards at 7.30am. Capt RICHARDS RAMC T.P. wounded while out at 8hrs, 30R wounded outside Becam.	André
"	2.7.16		Visited CARNOY 7.30am + 2.30pm at 12noon while hurt cleared. Advanced posts in and about dressing of wounded. Pretenders & we in electric with Coy B and posts Divisional original general. Pretenders & we on leave in contact according to ADMS IR Division men being kept clear by our bearers. Reported during night, intense barrage of enemy shrapnel making contact... to evacuate stretcher cases a few am. wounded of wounded German prisoners... 4 W Division for 2 days up to A.D.S. (initial dressings etc.) 5 years seven hurt... up the A.D.S. 447 cases $86/4$ slightly wounded... 47 Ω Ω 8 $6\phi5^{ewe}$ = 1355 Evacuation 6.0am 1st - 6.0am 2nd other unit stretcher up 18th Division $\frac{1}{5}$ H $\frac{1}{2}$ O.R 1 wounded 30th Division but Walking received & sent received	Distro

1875 Wt. W.593/826 4,000,000 4/15 J.B.C. & A. A.D.S.S./Forms/C.2118.
55 7A OR 1 wounded
Casualties

Army Form C. 2118

WAR DIARY
or
INTELLIGENCE SUMMARY
(Erase heading not required.)

MWinter 57A. Vol 13

Map ALBERT
Combined sheet 1/40,000

Instructions regarding War Diaries and Intelligence Summaries are contained in F. S. Regs., Part II. and the Staff Manual respectively. Title Pages will be prepared in manuscript.

Place	Date	Hour	Summary of Events and Information	Remarks and references to Appendices
L.10.c.1.1	3.7.16		18th Divisional front quiet. Visited CARNOY + left of village held by 18th Division). Now busy evacuation of MONTAUBAN section, in conjunction with R.M.service stretcher carrying. 7 wheeled & Ford cars to CARNOY, road not passable for Ford cars beyond gold German trenches. Casualties 55 7.A. O.R. 3 wounded of whom 2 remain at duty. Indeed Bowen Division 54 7.A. back into reserve at GROVETOWN camp (railway)	Appx
"	4.7.16		All quiet. Visited CARNOY now running in CARNOY, MAMETZ road to left plank & then up grass track to see what was no man's land. To which most cases are brought by hand.	Appx
"	5.7.16		Showed ADMS + BADMS 3rd Division RRONZAY, CARNOY + MONTAUBAN at latter place ADMS 3rd Div wanted a seller or other suitable place for collecting pt. Village is in ruins & no such place available. Road to MONTAUBAN improving slowly, not yet fit for motor transport beyond its line old German front the road has been badly cut up by transport in the events the front very quiet. Following wire 5/7 recd from 13th corps. Transmitted 18th Division + Transmitted. The Commander in chief directs me to convey to you + through you to the Directors + all concerned under them his high appreciation of their hard work & the efficiency of arrangements for dealing with the medical aspect of the present entire AAA 9th 18th 30th LDMS	Appx
"	6.7.16		Quiet day. Visited CARNOY	Appx

1875 Wt: W593/826 1,000,000 4/15 J.B.C. & A. A.D.S.S./Forms/C. 2118.

Army Form C. 2118

WAR DIARY
or
INTELLIGENCE SUMMARY
(Erase heading not required.)

M/W inder 57A Vol 13

from ALBERT
contained sheet 10/10000

Place	Date	Hour	Summary of Events and Information	Remarks and references to Appendices
L.10.c.1.1.	7.7.16		All quiet on front. Took O.C. 142 T.A. 3rd Division up to CARNOY to see ADS's & retake over from 18th Division. Necessary orders issued.	Ayso
"	8.7.16		The arrangements for Beaver Division for the attack were as follows. The Beaver Division worked over the area which was divided up into 3 sectors. Evacuation was carried out by hand wheel stretchers light achieved up to TALUS BOISE assisted by hutte from Beaver Division 54 & 57 T.A. other hutte from these Divisions were drawing at AD stations & loading cars relaying cars came from the advanced Capt. LISTER. The Beaver worked or organised his plans in a most highly efficient manner. He mentions Capt. RICHARDS for the efficient way in which the cars allotted were cleared O.R. where wounded were evacuated. He lists specially good Sgt. ELLIS, PENINGROVE, SHREEVES, SAYERS, HALL A., GARVEY, TAYLOR, Cpls Rees LOOBEY A.C.F. CAPT. HARTGILL who was in charge of medical arrangements and was responsible for the evacuation of cases from that point was untiring in his interviews and his general arrangements were exceptionally good. This officer specially drew attention to the work done by two Huns medical orderlies CRONIN & CAMPION. He further states that the work done by Capt. CHAPMAN 547A was very good. Capt. BIGGS O.C. Beaver 567A mention of Sgt RIDING & Pte SPITTLE 3674 & for good work collecting wounded under shell fire W56659 PteDAVIES & 56668 DAVIES Casualties in officers remaining at duty 9 O.R. of whom 4 remained at duty twenty (1st-8)	Ayso

Army Form C. 2118

WAR DIARY or INTELLIGENCE SUMMARY

(Erase heading not required.)

Instructions regarding War Diaries and Intelligence Summaries are contained in F. S. Regs., Part II. and the Staff Manual respectively. Title Pages will be prepared in manuscript.

M/Winter 557A Vol 13
Mah ALBERT
Corrected sheet 40,000

Place	Date	Hour	Summary of Events and Information	Remarks and references to Appendices

Casualties XIII Corps July 1-4. 1916

	Formation	Officers Lying	Other Ranks Walking	Other Ranks Lying	18 Division	Daily Totals by Formation 30 Division	Corps Troops & Other Divisions	Prisoners
1	18th Div	1	105	—	105			
	30" "	—	46	1		46		52
	Corps Troops Other Divisions	—	52	1				
2	18th Division	55	800	541	1396			
	30th "	106	629	1150		1885		276
	Corps Troops & Other Divisions	—	276	—				
3	18th Division	4	24	406	434			
	30th "	23	70	904		1687		60
	Corps Troops & Other Divisions	1	24	35				
4	18th Division	8	—	147	155			
	30th Division	8	—	1062		1070		1
	Corps Troops & Other Divisions	1	—	1				
Total		205	2026	4335	2090	4088	388	360

? about 600 walking Wounded unaccounted for. Grand Total 6926

Headquarters of 18 Station hitter moved to Main Dressing station in relieving 142 Field ambulance. Bearer division to return in 9th 18th Division. Killed in action 18th Division 632 ?

L.10.e.1.1 8/7/16

J 24

Army Form C. 2118

WAR DIARY
or
INTELLIGENCE SUMMARY
(Erase heading not required.)

Instructions regarding War Diaries and Intelligence Summaries are contained in F.S. Regs., Part II. and the Staff Manual respectively. Title Pages will be prepared in manuscript.

M/W mde   55 7A Vol 13

map ALBERT
(Confidential sheet)

Place	Date	Hour	Summary of Events and Information	Remarks and references to Appendices
T 24	9.7.16		Beaver division reported 10 hm. at	
"	10.7.16		Kit & equipment inspection	
"	11.7.16		Reequipped men with clothing etc	
"	12.7.16		Lt ELWOOD rejoined from 2/C.C.S. Capt SANDERS detailed for temporary duty at 21 C.C.S	
"	13.7.16		Beaver division buffer 21 ordered to GROVETOWN Camp in reserve	
"	14.7.16		Stretcher squad on Lt ELWOOD from 0/C 21 CCS forwarded to O/C RAMC 18th Division. Lt ELWOOD to Divisional Field Ambulance. Beaver division to MARICOURT 9.0am	
MARICOURT	14.7.16	1.15 pm	Hqs to MARICOURT. Transport & Quar remained at T 24. Capt YATES detached for temporary duty with X Force.	
"	15.7.16		Carrying out 24 hours relief with 54 A.D.S. Beavers 54, 55, 56 totaling 12 bearer teams of duty. Quiet.	
"	16.7.16		Quiet. Routine.	
"	17.7.16		Operation order A.D.M.S. ordered to take over charge of medical arrangements for division from 5/7A. who were in charge. Interim artillery to them	
"	18.7.16		Action to take over morning of 18th postponed 24 hours. Later postponed to a future date. 53 Inf Bde detached to work under 9th Division; detached Bearer division 86 7A to be attached. This to meet artillery arrangements of 9th Division	
"	19.7.16		Lt CUTHBERT posted temporary duty 11th Royal Fusiliers. Bombs at scheme of operations made by. from LONGUEVAL & DELVILLE WOOD. 55 7A Bearer division relieved by 106 7A Bearer	
"	20.7.16		L.H. A.D.S. MARICOURT to become 106 7A. Last division of this unit about 11.0 a.m. at 9.30 pm. Beaver not arrived 11.0 a.	

Army Form C. 2118

WAR DIARY
or
INTELLIGENCE SUMMARY
(Erase heading not required.)

M/Winder 55 7A Vol 13

Maj ALBERT commanding W/s/ed 14/7/1900

Place	Date	Hour	Summary of Events and Information	Remarks and references to Appendices
T.24	20.7.16		Received 2.0 p.m. orders from ADMS that unit will move to reserve area on 21st. All H.T. to move on 20th. Horse transport sent 5.0 p.m.	Appx
"	21.7.16		7.A. entrained MEAULTE to proceed to HUCHENNEVILLE via 14 M.A.C ABBEVILLE. Unit arrived 9.30 p.m. & went into billets. Ambulance remains closed.	Appx Appx Appx
HUCHENNEVILLE	22.7.16		Rest	Appx Appx
"	23.7.16		7.A. entrained for neighbourhood of ST OMER.	Appx Appx
CAMPAGNE	24.7.16		Detrained STONER & marched to CAMPAGNE. Map Belgium 3A	
"	25.7.16		Capt HARTGILL to Hq Division last night temporary duty as D.A.D.M.S. Capt LISTER proso + St ELLIS RAMC submitted again in connection the names of Capt RICHARDS & same for good work at TRONES wood. with TRONES WOOD. (Capt RICHARDS in same for good work in clearing TRONES WOOD.) The following names are noted for good work in connection. (HIGGS RAINBOW.) Pte POUT SHREEVES KEY. G. HALL A. WINGROVE SAYERS. EDWARDS E. These in brackets to be brought forward when called for.	Appx Appx
"	26.7.16		Belongs to 2nd Army. Rest LT DAWES RAME T.E. joined taken on strength. A hm for field of 55th Inf Bde. operation orders A.D.M.S. to move to HONDEGHEM area	Appx
"	27.7.16		7A m for field of 55th Inf Bde. operation orders 29th under orders of G.O.C 55th Inf Bde. 28th and to FLÊTRE arrived & billeted for night	Appx Appx
LE BREARDE	28.7.16		arrived 4.30 p.m. Remain closed till further orders	Appx
FLÊTRE	29.7.16		Closed	Appx
"	30.7.16		Closed	Appx
"	31.7.16			Appx

No. 55 Field Ambulance

18th Div

August 1916

WAR DIARY or INTELLIGENCE SUMMARY

Army Form C. 2118

557A
M Winter
Vol 14

MAP: HAZEBROUCK 5A. Belgium & France Sheet 36

Place	Date	Hour	Summary of Events and Information	Remarks and references to Appendices
FLÊTRE	1.8.16		Operation Order from A.D.M.S. Division taken over (sheet 36) from 1/2 Division. 557A to take over evacuation from 10.0 p.m. 1st A. Advance parties 2nd main body 3rd. Main dressing station FORT. ROMPU. A.D.S. ERQUINGHEM. collecting posts 2 (1) Brickfields at I.18.a.9.1. (2) BOIS GRENIER, in Brewery cellar H.24.d.2.4. C.C.S. at TROIS ARBRES. Divisional first ccav to DOULIEU	Antra
"	2.8.16		Advance parties to FORT ROMPU + ERQUINGHEM arrived later. Place + BOIS GRENIER. Collecting post.	Antra
"	3.8.16		F.G.C.M. Pte THORNTON under Sec 9(a) A.A. on 27th ult. 3 months F.S.P. no 1 promulgated this day. Visited FORT. ROMPU.	Antra
FORT.ROMPU.	4.8.16		3rd year of war. 7A moved to FORT. ROMPU arriving 9.30 a.m. Routine to complete A.D.S. a O.Ps. left at 8.30 a.m. notified A.D.M.S. complete. Receiving from 12 noon.	Antra
"	5.8.16		1 officer 20 O.R. admitted. 1 officer 10 O.R. to C.C.S. remain 10	Antra
"	6.8.16		2 officers 30 O.R. admitted including 9 wounded (1 offr) 1 offr 13 O.R. to C.C.S. 1 offr 19 O.R. remain	
"	7.8.16		2 officers 31 O.R. admitted including 17 wounded. 1 offr 17 O.R. to C.C.S. 2 offr 10 R.T.A.D.R. 29 remain	
"	8.8.16		Visited O.P. at I.18.a.9.1. + A.D.S. ERQUINGHEM yesterday, also regtl aid post of Lpt.sector. 1 offr 45 O.R. admitted including 17 wounded 2 offrs C.C.S. 8 to Div 40 remaining	Antra

WAR DIARY or INTELLIGENCE SUMMARY

Army Form C. 2118
Vol 14

Place	Date	Hour	Summary of Events and Information	Remarks and references to Appendices
FORT. ROMPU	9.8.16		Map Squared BELGIUM + FRANCE Sheet 36.	
			admitted 10/Офр 20 O.R. including 1 Офр 2 O.R. wounded 1 Офр 8 O.R. to duty. 4 1 O.R. remain	AntPo
"	10.8.16		Visited A.D.S. & BOIS GRENIER also R.A.P. and 1 Right Flank	AntPo
			admitted 2 Офр 31 O.R. 2 Офр 13 O.R. to duty 57 remain	AntPo
"	11.8.16		1 Officer 16 O.R. admitted 1 Офр 4 O.R. to duty 8 to D.R. 55 remain	AntPo
At	12.8.16		31 admissions. 2 Officers 5 to C.C.S. 9 to D.R. 70 remain	AntPo
			Visited A.D.S. & C.P. with A.D.M.S.	
"	13.8.16		admitted 27 O.R. including 5 wounded. 11 to C.C.S. 18 to D.R. 2 died 5 to duty 63 remain	AntPo
"	14.8.16		2 Офр 25 O.R. admitted 1 Офр 13 O.R. to C.C.S. 10 Офр 11 O.R. to D.R. 8 to duty 59 remain	AntPo
"	15.8.16		2 Офр 40 O.R. admitted including 10 wounded 2 Офр 16 O.R. to C.C.S. 21 to D.R.S. 2 died 48 remain	AntPo
"	16.8.16		11 admissions including 3 wounded 10 to C.C.S. 9 to D.R. 43 remain	AntPo
			Visited A.D.S.	
"	17.8.16		14 admissions. 6 to C.C.S. 19 to D.R. 31 remain.	AntPo
"	18.8.16		20 admissions including 4 wounded. 10 to C.C.S. 5 to D.R. 1 died 33 remain.	AntPo
"	19.8.16		10 admissions 4 to C.C.S. 15 D.R. 28 remain.	AntPo
			Officers & orders from A.D.M.S. hand over to 102 F.A. to be completed 22nd, & then move to ESTAIRES. Visited A.D.S.	AntPo
"	20.8.16		15 admissions. 2 to C.C.S. 2 to D.R. 38 remain 102.F.A. arrived to take over.	AntPo
"	21.8.16		2 Офр 24 O.R. admitted 1 Офр 9 O.R. to C.C.S. 12 to D.R. 1 Офр 40 R. to duty 37 remain.	AntPo
"	22.8.16		C.P. & A.D.S. handed over to 102.F.A. Hand over to 102.F.A. — marched to ESTAIRES. 10.30 am Motor Transport left behind by order of G.H.Q.	AntPo
ESTAIRES	23.8.16			AntPo

Army Form C. 2118

Vol 14

557A
map LENS, 11

WAR DIARY
or
INTELLIGENCE SUMMARY
(Erase heading not required.)

Place	Date	Hour	Summary of Events and Information	Remarks and references to Appendices
ESTAIRES	24.8.16		Resting	apps
TINQUETTE	25.8.16		Entrained & moved to TINQUETTE map LENS, 11. 6 miles S of ST. POL. B'llets indifferent.	apps
"	26.8.16		Opened for patients up to 30 in a large hut.	apps
"	27.8.16		No patients, cleaning up area	apps
"	28.8.16		3 cases remaining. LT STEWART. R.B. RAME T.C. joined for duty & taken on strength	apps
"	29.8.16		10 cases remain. LT DAWES to Base & struck off strength accordingly. Rain	apps
"	30.8.16		15 admissions, 6 to ccs, 18 remain. Much rain.	apps
"	31.8.16		9 admissions 26 remain	apps

140/184

18th Div.

55th Field Ambulance.

COMMITTEE FOR THE
MEDICAL HISTORY OF THE WAR
Date -9 DEC. 1915

A.D.M.S.
  18th Division

War Diary 557A for September 1916
forwarded in accordance with
18th DRO No 522 of 15/7/16
Please acknowledge.

1/10/16

M Winder
Lt Col RAMC
O C 557A

WAR DIARY
INTELLIGENCE SUMMARY

Army Form C. 2118

55 F.A.
Major Winder
Vol 15

Major LENS H.

Place	Date	Hour	Summary of Events and Information	Remarks and references to Appendices
TINQUETTE	1.9.16		10/fr 6.O.R. admitted 1/fr 3.O.R. to C.C.S. 7 to duty 22 remain	
"	2.9.16		2 off 13 O.R. admitted 1/fr 6 O.R. to C.C.S. 2 off 24 O.R. remain	
"	3.7.16		7 admissions, 2 officers 8 o.r. to C.C.S. 19 remain	
"			Received operation order A.D.M.S. Division to march to new area transferred to Reserve army. March 5th 6th 7th made arrangements with 55th I.B.	
"	4.9.16		10/fr 11 O.R. admitted 10/fr 8 O.R. to C.C.S. 20 remain. Brigade orders received for march. New march order issued	
"	5.9.16		2 off 38 O.R. admitted 2 off 46 O.R. to C.C.S. to duty 8 remain, a number of these cases were trivial cases dumped on Regt before moving. Another 15 were referred to admin. & returned to their Amb. O. order received at 2.0 a.m. cancelling the	
"			move till further orders	
"	6.9.16		10 admissions. 18 remain	
"	7.9.16		5 admissions 5 to C.C.S. 18 remain	
"	8.9.16		10/fr 12 O.R. admitted 10/fr 5 O.R. to C.C.S. 22 remain. Received orders for move on 9th, int some move an order on 4th	
HOUVIN HOUVIGNEUL	9.9.16		Marched with 55th Inf Bde. evacuated 2 officers 32 or to C.C.S. 2 o.r. remain	
LUCHEUX	10.9.16		Marched with 55th Inf Bde evacuated 11 to C.C.S. 2 remain	
PUCHEVILLERS	11.9.16		Belong to IInd Corps Reserve army from midnight 10/11 Marched with 55th Inf Bde.	
"	12.9.16		evacuated 18 to C.C.S. 2 remain 3 admissions 4 remain	
"	13.9.16		8 admissions 3 to C.C.S. 9 remain	

WAR DIARY
or
INTELLIGENCE SUMMARY

(Erase heading not required.)

Army Form C. 2118

35 F.A.
Vol 15

Map LENS. 11

Place	Date	Hour	Summary of Events and Information	Remarks and references to Appendices
PUCHEVILLERS.	14.9.16		6 admissions 9 to eve. 5 remain	Appx
"	15.9.16		3 to duty 2 remain 1 to eve. 9 remain	Appx
"	16.9.16		9 admissions 1 to eve.	Appx
"	17.9.16		10/R 9 O.R. admitted 4 to eve. 10/R 14 O.R. remain Capt LISTER RAMC to ME ST ELLIS Dermat.	Appx
"	18.9.16		Rain. 5 admissions 10/R 6 O.R. to eve. 10 remain	Appx
"	19.9.16		Rain. 4 admissions 12 remain	Appx
"	20.9.16		Rain. 10/R 1 O.O. Admitted 3 to eve 10/R 17 O.R. remain	Appx
"	21.9.16		Rain. 5 admissions 10/R to duty 4 O.R. to eve. 17 remain Capt McKENZIE RAMC posted to 8th Rl Sussex Pioneers & took off strength	Appx
"	22.9.16		10/R 6 O.R. admitted 10/R 6 O.R. to eve 16 remain	Appx
"	23.9.16		9 admissions 1 to eve. 20 remain Operation orders from A.D.M.S. to move & Beaver division move & to MARTINSART VALLEY W of AVELUY Wood. Test division 1st to CLAIRFAYE FARM. Visited CLAIRFAYE FARM.	Appx
"	24.9.16		10/R 1 O.R. admitted 10/R 8 O.R. to eve. 4 remain Beaver division moved up as ordered to remain in reserve map reference ALBERT S5 Central W. 4 (a) (3) (2) Head qrs to CLAIRFAYE FARM. & took over dressing station including 60 cases, 8 wounded 59 remain	Appx
CLAIRFAYE FARM.	25.9.16		Arranged hospital marquee, pain reception & dressing. Again down cases, & had little in walking wounded. Visited Beaver division	Appx

Army Form C. 2118

53-7A.
Vol 15

WAR DIARY
or
INTELLIGENCE SUMMARY

(Erase heading not required.)

Ypres
Operations 11 — ALBERT 3y
consisted 1/5, 1916

Place	Date	Hour	Summary of Events and Information	Remarks and references to Appendices
CLAIRFAYE FARM	26.9.16		Admitted 3 offrs 96 OR including 25 wounded. 3 offrs 28 OR to C.C.S. 30 to duty remain 97. Attack on THIEPVAL at 12.30 pm Cases coming in from	
"	27.9.16	4.0 pm	admitted 10 sick + 9 wounded officers. Transferred to C.C.S.? 57 sick 443 wounded OR. Transferred 54 sick 360 wounded. 1 death. Remain 59 sick 103 wounded O.R. wounded include gunners 3 offrs 59 O.R.	
"	28.9.16		admitted 12 officers 368 OR including 287 wounded. 11 offrs 245 OR to C.C.S. Remain 1 offr 261 OR. Visited Ovillers	
"	29.9.16		admitted 14 offrs 566 OR including 87 wounded. 10 offrs 291 OR to C.C.S. wounded. 100 OR remain 2 offrs 395 O.R.	
"	30.9.16		admitted 15 officers including 13 wounded 16 to C.C.S. 1 remain 331 OR " 234 " 320 " 328 remain	

WAR DIARY or INTELLIGENCE SUMMARY

Army Form C. 2118

557A
NYWinter V/16
Maj LENS 11th ALBERT SE Comd

Place	Date	Hour	Summary of Events and Information	Remarks and references to Appendices
CLAIRFAYE FARM	1.10.16		Admitted 4 officers wounded 5 to CCS. " 359 OR including 301 wounded 176 to CCS. 446 remain. LT ELWOOD R.A.M.C. to 3rd Canadian Div. strength off strength 30.9.16	sgd
"	2.10.16		admitted 60 officers including 4 wounded to CCS remain 2. " 1230 OR including 88 wounded 229 to CCS remain 261	sgd
"	3.10.16		Capt A.H. JAMES R.A.M.C. to Div. Hospital taken on strength admitted 12 officers including 6 wounded 9 to CCS 5 remain " 226 OR " 162 " 168 to CCS 264 remain	sgd
"	4.10.16		admitted 7 officers including 4 wounded 10 to CCS 2 remain " 229 OR " 88 " 199 to CCS 240 remain wounded 27 " 155 to CCS 4a. temporarily to 133 SA, 67A attached per man. 330 IR including 4a. temporarily to 133 SA, 67A and remain. hauled over at 1.30pm the equipment etc. to 133 SA. Advance party by train to take over new area at 71 ENVILLERS near CANDAS 557A div beaver division arrived 2.30pm. Beaver division + motor transport remain attached to 567A	sgd
71 ENVILLERS	5.10.16			
"	6.10.16		Period 26.9 to 4.10 Casualties through h.ds were as follows. Wounded officers 44 OR 1130 18th Div Sick " 5 OR 320 18th Div " 12 " 280 other Div 16 " 472 other Div ____ 212 German 17 600 60 — 2114 Beaver Division rejoined 9.0 pm	sgd

WAR DIARY
or
INTELLIGENCE SUMMARY
(Erase heading not required.)

Army Form C. 2118

Vol. 16

No. 557A

Place	Date	Hour	Summary of Events and Information	Remarks and references to Appendices
FIENVILLERS	7.10.16		Opened up accommodation for 20 patients. Casualties at HIERVAL. Ptes SHREEVES & WALLACE J. Died 1.10.16 WILLIS A.W. 30.9.16. Pte HUGHES J.R. HENDERSON J. TAPPIN L.W. MANFORD Z. GIFFORD. Pt TATTERSAL wounded & evacuated. Pte POUT. THOMAS J.T. HALL N.M. TAYLOR W.E. FAIRLESS ST. ELLIS. S/SGT GUEST. Pt POTTINGTON. Pt BIRKINSHAW. LEATHERS. KNOCKER. MORRIS H.B. wounded remain at duty.	Appx
"	8.10.16		Report from Capt LISTER O.C. Bearers commendi especially Pte HALL N.M. THORNTON. BERRY. Pte SAYERS. KIRBYSON. FAIRLESS. L/CPL TAYLOR H. Pte POUT. KEY. S. KNOCKER. LAWES. 9 (LT. STEWART. (M.B.) submitted above to ADMS submitted recommendation for his name to ADMS	Appx / Appx
"	9.10.16		3 patients	Appx
"	10.10.16		14 admissions 4 to ccs 13 remain	Appx
"	11.10.16		admitted 10 offrs 1 IOR 6 to duty 10 offrs 8 OR remain admissions 4. 10 offrs 1 OR to ccs 6 remain	Appx / Appx
"	12.10.16		admissions 9 remain 13	Appx
"	13.10.16		admissions 10 offrs 8 OR. 14 offrs 3 OR to ccs 9 remain. Rain. LT STEWART awaye sick returned from ADMS	Appx
"	14.10.16		for visit to move up with 55 D/ Side.	Appx
BRETEL	15.10.16		Reported around. admissions 2 offrs 21 OR to ccs 2 offrs 31 OR nil remain	Appx
RUBEMPRÉ	16.10.16		arrived 5.0 pm reported to ADMS + A.055 44 55th 2nd ride	Appx

Army Form C. 2118

WAR DIARY
or
INTELLIGENCE SUMMARY
(Erase heading not required.)

Vol 16

M/Winter 55 7A

Maj. LEWIS, 1/ Albert Cambrelshef/3 ADS

Place	Date	Hour	Summary of Events and Information	Remarks and references to Appendices
ALBERT	17.10.16		Arrived 3.30 pm. Bivouaced on outskirts of town. Reported arrival ADMS 55 Div. Saw ADMS who explained that 55 Div had hurriedly no accommodation tentage or bivouac & informed him that under the circumstances wet & cold weather I should refuse to accept any sick from the brigades & require my own tentage for my own personnel.	Appx
"	18.10.16		Visited ADS POZIERES with ADMS. One germans dug out, one splinter proof divisn room. Take about 3/4 stretch & stretcher afterwards covered over a round keyed for personnel resting.	Appx Appx Appx Appx
"	19.10.16		nil	
"	20.10.16		Visited POZIERES	
"	21.10.16		nil	
"	22.10.16			
LA BOISELLE	23.10.16		Moved into billets position. Hq LA.BOISELLE. ADS party POZIERES Lewis Division R 28.d.6.8 / 54 F.A. Beaver division Bay R 29 central moving to lack of protection only shelter hutes east in front of LA BOISELLE will have from.	Appx
"	24.10.16		nil	
"	25.10.16		have deferred till 28th. Visited 29 central Tram system, POZIERES to 29 central mountain position. Wanted names to ADMS.	Appx
"	26.10.16		Summary evidence against Sgt BANCB HT ASC. Refusing to obey an order	Appx

WAR DIARY
~~INTELLIGENCE~~ SUMMARY

(Erase heading not required.)

Army Form C. 2118

557A
Vol 16

Place	Date	Hour	Summary of Events and Information	Remarks and references to Appendices
LA BOISELLE	27.10.16		Ptes SAYERS, FAIRLESS, T/Lt TAYLOR H, Pte LAWES, KIRBYSON, POUT, KNOCKER recommended	
"	28.10.16		Military medals recommended 8.10.16	
"	29.10.16		Nil	
"	30.10.16		Took ADMS + DDMS to ADS POZIERES. Rain	
"	31.10.16		Rain (nil)	
			Total Casualties 557A O.R. one wounded	

14th Div.

No. 55 Field Ambulance.

Nov 1916

COMMITTEE FOR THE
MEDICAL HISTORY OF THE WAR
Date -3 JAN. 1917

WAR DIARY
or
INTELLIGENCE SUMMARY
(Erase heading not required.)

Army Form C. 2118

MMingle 557A Vol 17

ALBERT SW Bombard 1/40,000 Vol 17

Place	Date	Hour	Summary of Events and Information	Remarks and references to Appendices
LA BOISELLE	1-11-16		Visited POZIERES 28 & 29 central adv posts.	
"	2-11-16		Nil	
"	3-11-16		Nil	
"	4-11-16		Operations delayed	
"	5-11-16		Nil	
"	6-11-16		Lt BULL RAMC posted to 88 Adv RTA & struck off strength	
"	7-11-16		Capt LISTER has to relieve from Pts THORNTON & BERRY Distinguished conduct med & Pt HALLUM military medal	
"	8-11-16		Nil	
"	9-11-16		Nil	
"	10-11-16		Nil	
"	11-11-16		Nil	
"	12-11-16		moved to 54 & 55 Beaver divisions into position. Visited POZIERES. Battle with d RANGEE 1ST Division not engaged	
"	13-11-16		Lt T.W. JACKSON RAMC to reported & taken on strength	
"	14-11-16		Operations postponed	
"	15-11-16		Operations postponed till further notice	
"	16-11-16		Nil	
"	17-11-16		Beaver divisions to battle position. 54 & 55 leaven from 29 central to gravel pit having been altered. Evacuation from there thro near MOUQUET FARM. owing to line	
"			DONNETS POST. Ly them thence by motor Ambulance to ALBERT thro AVELUY. Small postponed on a dummy attack at DONNETS POST	
"	18-11-16	6.10am	attack. DESIRE TRENCH taken. About 250 cases in all evacuated	
"	19-11-16			

Army Form C. 2118

WAR DIARY
or
INTELLIGENCE SUMMARY
(Erase heading not required.)

VOL 17

Army November 57A

Place	Date	Hour	Summary of Events and Information	Remarks and references to Appendices
LA BOISELLE	20.11.16		ABBEVILLE — LENS / 130,000 — ALBERT / 40,000 — All quiet, reduced strengths of bearers 56/7A leaving relieved 54/7A bearers	MJC
"	21.11.16		Handed over the front to Ambulance 61st division & withdrew to ALBERT	AG/JC
VADENCOURT	22.11.16		Marched to VADENCOURT, arrived in the dark, march difficult	AG/JC
FIENVILLERS	23.11.16		Arrived 7.30 pm. Good billets	AG/JC
"	24.11.16		Resting. Recommended Capt RICHARDS for Military Cross. Sgt TAYLOR & Pte KEY for military medal	AG/JC
"	25.11.16		March	AG/JC
MAISON PONTHIEU	26.11.16		Arrived 14 mtrs. Opening 7A. for 30 bearers	AG/JC
JOMVAST	27.11.16		Open for Brigade sick 7.30 PM. on Sgt RANGE MT & SE	AG/JC
ABBEVILLE	28.11.16		Lt Col hinde proceeded to H.Q. 18 Div as acting ADMS	KCA
"	29.11.16		Capt. WILLIAM HENRY LASLETT R.A.M.C. T.C. reported for duty, & taken on strength. Admitted 9. Duty 1. Remain 8	KCA
"	30.11.16		Admitted 11. Duty 1. evacuated 2. Remain 17 — Heavy Frost. Second blankets issued to men	KCA

140/1903.

COMMITTEE FOR THE
MEDICAL HISTORY OF THE WAR
Date   31 JAN. 1917

18th Div.

55th Field Ambulance

Dec 1916

WAR DIARY or INTELLIGENCE SUMMARY

Army Form C. 2118

Y.A. 1st Army, 1st Division, 55 F.A. Vol. 18

ARGEUVILLE 100,000

Place	Date	Hour	Summary of Events and Information	Remarks and references to Appendices
DOMVAST	1.12.16		Admitted 1 officer 8 O.R. Evacuated 1 officer to No.2 Stat. Hosp. Duty 3 O.R. Remained 22. Sent to B.R.C.S. KECMESNIL Farm to draw oil stoves for heating wards - None in stock, nor likelihood of any. Lt. T.W. JACKSON posted on temporary M.O. i/c 7th E. KENTS.	b/cA
"	2.12.16		Admitted 1 officer 6 O.R. Evacuated 1 officer to No.2 Stat. Hosp. 7 O.R. Duty 1 O.R. Remained 20. Proceedings of F.G.C.M. on No M2/045694 Sgt. BANGE J. A.S.C. M.T. received for promulgation. Nil fault.	b/cA
			Capt. W.H. LISTER M.C. R.A.M.C.(T.C.) proceeded today to report to A.D.M.S. CALAIS & struck off strength. Capt. N.K. RICHARDS posted on temporary M.O. i/c 7th R.W. SURREYS.	
"	3.12.16		Admitted 4. Evacuated to Gratimann Hosp. 3. Transferred to 54 F.A. 3. Duty 1. Remained 17. Sentence promulgated in case of F.G.C.M. on M2/045694 Sgt. BANGE J. A.C. M.T.	b/cA
"	4.12.16		Admitted 7. Evacuated 3. Duty 2. Remained 19.	b/cA
"	5.12.16		Admitted 8. Evacuated 2. Duty 2 - Remained 23.	b/cA
"	6.12.16		Admitted 3. Evacuated 4. Duty 1 - Remained 21	b/cA
"	7.12.16		Admitted 6. Evacuated 4. Duty 4 - Remained 17 — Capt. E.S. CUTHBERT R.A.M.C. T.F. posted as M.P. i/c 12th MIDDLESEX & struck off strength. D.D.M.S. II Corps inspected the 3rd Fd. Ambulance area & hospital	b/cA
"	8.12.16		Admitted 5. Duty 3. Remained 22.	b/cA
"	9.12.16		Admitted 13. Evacuated 6. Duty 4. Remained 21. D.M.S. 5th Army inspected Fd. Amb. & Hospital. Capt. P.G. BELINGER R.A.M.C. S.R. posted on duty & taken on strength.	b/cA
"	10.12.16		Admitted 4. Evacuated 4. Duty 1. Remained 23.	b/cA
"	11.12.16		Admitted 1 officer 6 O.R. Evacuated 1 officer 3 O.R. Duty 1 - Remained 17	b/cA
"	12.12.16		Admitted 1. Evacuated 5. Duty 2. Remained 21. Heavy fall of snow	b/cA
"	13.12.16		Admitted 1 officer 7 O.R. Evacuated 1 officer 3 O.R. Duty 5 - Remained 28. Lt.Col. WINDER returned from A.D.M.S. 19 Divl. H.Q.	b/cA
"	14.12.16		Admitted 13. Evacuated 4. Duty 2. Remained 29.	b/cA
"			Admitted 1 officer 16 O.R. Evacuated 1 officer 5 O.R. Duty 4. Remained 29.	b/cA

WAR DIARY or INTELLIGENCE SUMMARY

Army Form C. 2118

ABBEVILLE 5571A

Place	Date	Hour	Summary of Events and Information	Remarks and references to Appendices
BONVAST	15/12/16		13 admitted 6 evacuated 27 remain	
"	16/12/16		8 admitted 3 evacuated 25 remain	
"	17/12/16		6 admitted 9 evacuated 20 remain	
"	18/12/16		6 admitted 2 evacuated 16 remain	
"	19/12/16		10 admitted 3 evacuated 22 remain	
"	20/12/16		10 admitted 4 evacuated 28 remain	
"	21/12/16		10/th S.O.R. admitted 10/th S.O.R. evacuated 30 remain	
"	22/12/16		5 admitted 3 evacuated 25 remain	
"	23/12/16		3 admitted 6 evacuated 19 remain. Lt.Col. M.G. WINDER proceeded on leave 23/12 - 2/1	W.E.A.
"	24/12/16		4 admitted 5 evacuated 14 remain.	h.C.A.
"	25/12/16		3 admitted 5 evacuated 9 remain	h.C.A.
"	26/12/16		5 admitted 0 evacuated 13 remain	h.C.A.
"	27/12/16		7 admitted 5 evacuated 13 remain	h.C.A.
"	28/12/16		3 admitted 6 evacuated 9 remaining - Capt. P.B. BELANGER proceeded on 6 weeks leave to CANADA	h.C.A.
"	29/12/16		5 admitted 1 evacuated 11 remain	h.C.A.
"	30/12/16		23 admitted 8 evacuated 24 remain	h.C.A.
"	31/12/16		6 admitted 4 evacuated 22 remain. D.A.D.M.S. II Corps inspected Hospital	h.C.A.

140/99 M

18th Div

55th Field Ambulance

Jan. 1917

WAR DIARY
or
INTELLIGENCE SUMMARY
(Erase heading not required.)

Army Form C. 2118

55 Field Amb.
Minutes in Charge
Vol. 19

Instructions regarding War Diaries and Intelligence Summaries are contained in F.S. Regs., Part II. and the Staff Manual respectively. Title Pages will be prepared in manuscript.

Place	Date	Hour	Summary of Events and Information	Remarks and references to Appendices
			Map. ABBEVILLE 1/80,000 LENS 1/40,000 Vol 19	
DOMVAST	1.1.17		10 Admitted 5 Evacuated 26 Remaining. Lt.Col. M.G. WINDER awarded D.S.O.	Initials
"	2.1.17		15 Admitted 7 Evacuated 32 Remain. London Gazette published in connection with New Year's Honours List.	Initials
"	3.1.17		12 admitted 6 evacuated 37 remain. Capt W.E. HARTGILL awarded M.C.	Initials
"	4.1.17		9 admitted 8 evacuated 37 remain.	Initials
"	5.1.17		13 admitted 4 evacuated 36 remain	Initials
"	6.1.17		8 admitted 5 evacuated 36 remain admissions include 6 bombing accident	Initials
"	7.1.17		8 admitted 3 evacuated 33 remain. 1 case O.S.M. in evacuation	Initials
"	8.1.17		3 admitted 4 evacuated 28 remain. Corps Commander inspected transport	Initials
"	9.1.17		17 admitted 4 evacuated 39 remain	Initials
"	10.1.17		12 admitted 13 evacuated 35 remain 9 to DRS.	Initials
"	11.1.17		Hospital closed 29 admitted 2 evacuated 62 remain. Marched to COULENVILLERS. mail received reported	Initials
COULENVILLERS	12.1.17		to ADMS. by 55 FA. 7 admitted 2 evacuated. Marched to LE MEILLARD arrival reported to 55 FA + ADMS	Initials
LE MEILLARD	13.1.17		no march no admissions	Initials
"	14.1.17		22 admissions 22 evacuated. Marched to BEAUQUESNE 2 offr 30 o.r. to FOREVILLE advance party	Initials
BEAUQUESNE	15.1.17		March to FOREVILLE + took over Corps rest/bus station with patients 2 offr 332 o.r. 19 Offr 200 O Capt'd Large huts + left over officers + bell tents	Initials
FOREVILLE	16.1.17		accommodation 3 large huts with normal capacity 395. 14 admitted − 2 offr 335 o.r remain Visited admitted	Initials
"	17.1.17		21 admitted 94 discharge 2 offr 262 o.r. remain visited DDMS re cord, oil + laundry	Initials
"	18.1.17		2 offr 350 O.R. admitted. 37 discharge 4 offr 260 O.R. remain. DDMS inspected	Initials
"	19.1.17		300 R admitted 14 offr 510 R to duty. 3 offr 239 o.r. remain	Initials

Army Form C. 2118

WAR DIARY
or
INTELLIGENCE SUMMARY
(Erase heading not required.)

Vol 19

55 7A m/under
LENS 1/(00,000)

Place	Date	Hour	Summary of Events and Information	Remarks and references to Appendices
FORCEVILLE	20.1.17		2.0 admitted 34 to duty 30 off 224 O.R. remain. Visited Calotard. Handed over	Anfro
"	21.1.17		Calotard to 56 7A	
"	22.1.17		8 admitted 31 to duty 3 off 200 O.R. remain	Anfro
"	23.1.17		24 admitted 32 to duty 3 off 192 O.R. remain. Frost.	Anfro
"	24.1.17		20 off 21 O.R. admitted 27 to duty 5 off 186 O.R. remain. Hard frost. Token lorry frozen.	Anfro
"	25.1.17		25 admitted 10 off 32 O.R. to duty 4 off 178 O.R. remain. DDMS inspected V.H. post	Anfro
"	26.1.17		12 admitted 41 to duty 4 off 149 O.R. remain. V.H. post	Anfro
"	27.1.17		15 admitted 31 to duty 4 off 133 O.R. remain. V.H. post 10 off 25 O.R. working party to 39	Anfro
"	28.1.17		10 admitted 10 off 19 O.R. to duty 3 off 124 remain. V.H. post	Anfro
"	29.1.17		14 admitted 10 off 20 O.R. to duty 20 off 118 O.R. remain V.H. post. Token thawed 9½ day	Anfro
"	30.1.17		10 off 17 O.R. admitted 24 to duty 30 off 110 O.R. remain V.H. post Token frozen hard	Anfro
"	31.1.17		17 admitted 22 to duty 3 off 105 O.R. remain V.H. post. snow	Anfro
"			20 off 22 O.R. admitted 8 to duty 5 off 118 O.R. remain V.H. post. snow	Anfro
			DDMS inspected	

140/994

18th Div.

55th Field Ambulance.

COMMITTEE FOR THE
MEDICAL HISTORY OF THE WAR
Date 4 — APR. 1917

WAR DIARY or **INTELLIGENCE SUMMARY**

Army Form C. 2118

Vol 20

V.57.A

LENS 1/100,000

Place	Date	Hour	Summary of Events and Information	Remarks and references to Appendices
FORCEVILLE	1.2.17		Admitted 15 - 1 Offr 14 OR to duty 4 Offr 117 OR remain. Working party 21 OR. DS 54 ?A Forge head post.	Antro
"	2.2.17		Admitted 6. 23 to duty.	Antro
"	3.2.17		Admitted 24. 10 Offr 15 OR to duty. 3 Offr 108 OR remain. V.H. post D.M.S. inspected.	Antro
"	4.2.17		Admitted 24. 26 to duty 4 Offr 101 OR remain. V.H. post	Re Marshall
"	5.2.17		Admitted 10. 12 to duty. 3 Offr 101 OR remain. 4 Col WINDER to Div Hq as acty A.D.M.S.	h.C.A.
"	6.2.17		Admitted 10. 13 to duty. 3 Offr 98 OR remain. V.H. post ADMS inspected	h.C.A.
"	7.2.17		Admitted 15. 2 Offrs 4 OR to duty 1 Offr 102 OR remain. V.H. post	h.C.A.
"	8.2.17		Admitted 8. 13 to duty. 1 Offr 93 OR remain. Visited VADENCOURT with view to taking over	h.C.A.
"	9.2.17		Admitted 6. 21 to duty. 1 Offr 78 OR remain. V.H. post	h.C.A.
"	10.2.17		Admitted 15. 18 to duty 1 Offr 74 OR remain. V.H. post II Corps "A" inspected	h.c.A.
"	11.2.17		Admitted 12. 6 to duty 1 Offr 79 OR remain. V.H. post ADMS inspected	h.C.A.
"	12.2.17		Admitted 14. 1 Offr 7 OR to duty 86 OR remain. V.H. post - inclined to thaw	h.C.A.
"	13.2.17		Admitted 1 Offr 24 OR. 11 OR to duty. 1 Offr 96 OR remain. Attended conference re Ambce Commander at A.D.M.S. Office Party 6 OR detailed to hold Rest station at WARLOY.	h.C.A.
"	14.2.17		Admitted 16. 13 to duty. 1 Offr 94 OR remain - slight thaw	h.C.A.
"	15.2.17		Admitted 15. 28 to duty. 1 Offr 85 OR remain.	h.C.A.
"	16.2.17		Admitted 30. 9 to duty 1 Offr 106 OR remain - Party 30 OR to form up hill machine putties under Capt GATLEY	h.C.A.
			attached to 54 F.A. Two completing Bearer Divs under Capt. RICHARDS - 2 Offrs 99 OR.	
"	17.2.17		Admitted 12. 30 to duty. 1 Offr 86 OR remain.	h.C.A.
"	18.2.17		Admitted 10 Offr 90 OR. 17 to duty. 1 Offr to C.C.S. 1 Offr 76 OR remain.	h.C.A.
"	19.2.17		Admitted 21. 12 to duty. 1 Offr 85 OR remain.	Antro

WAR DIARY
or
INTELLIGENCE SUMMARY
(Erase heading not required.)

Army Form C. 2118

55-7A Vol 20
M/Winder

LENS 1/100,000

Place	Date	Hour	Summary of Events and Information	Remarks and references to Appendices
FOREEVILLE	20.2.17		admitted 8, to duty 1 death. Case brought in moribund (broncho pneumonia) 10/ff 81.OR remain	
"	21.2.17		3 offr 17.O.R. admitted 10/ff 30.OR to duty, remain 2 offr 59.OR. Capt SANDERS 55-7A evacuated to e.c.S with ? hand gland.	
			Moved at FOREVILLE & opened Chateau VADENCOURT on IInd Corps Sealing station, equipment brought across 5th Corps not take over. Foreville expected to take all equipment	
VADENCOURT	22.2.17		11 admitted - 2 offr 70 OR remain ^ D.M.S. inspected	
"	23.2.17		17 admitted - 1 to duty - 2 offr 86.OR remain ADMS & DDMS inspected	
"	24.2.17		10 offr 5.O.R. admitted 3 offr 91.O.R remain 1 offr 15.O.R. refitted from no 2 TA. RNDivision & posted for duty at offrs Hospital WARLOY	
"	25.2.17		10 admitted 4 to duty 3 offr 96.OR. remain officers transferred to Hospital WARLOY this Hospital being run from Hy 55-74.	
"	26.2.17		21 admitted 10 to duty 3 offr 106 OR remain	
"	27.2.17		Capt BELANGER posted M.O X Ensign 26th Capt PENNY R.A.M.C.T.C. posted from X Ensign 26th & taken on strength.	
"	28.2.17		3 offr 8.O.R. admitted 10/ff to GEZAINCOURT. 35 OR to duty 5 offr 79 OR remain 4 offr 22 OR admitted 16 OR to duty 5 offr 84 OR remain 3 guns now relieve Sick officers as well as orders	

140/1024

COMMITTEE FOR THE
MEDICAL HISTORY OF THE WAR
Date   11 MAY. 1917

55th Field Ambulance.

Marshall

WAR DIARY
or
INTELLIGENCE SUMMARY

(Erase heading not required.)

Army Form C. 2118

Vol 21 55 F.A.

Place	Date	Hour	Summary of Events and Information ALBERT combined 40,000 / 100,000 LENS 1/100,000	Remarks and references to Appendices
VADENCOURT	1.3.17		O/fr 9 remained 2 adm 2 to duty 9 remain (2 oedine) O.R. 84 remained 20 adm 10 to duty 93 remain	
"	2.3.17		O/fr 9 remained 4 adm 13 remain O.R. 93 remained 12 adm 9 to duty 96 remain	
"	3.3.17		O/fr 1 admitted 14 remain arranged with O.C. 52 F.A. to hold over WARLOY O.R. 22 admitted 15 to duty 103 remain & VADENCOURT in accordance with instructions	
"	4.3.17		Handed over WARLOY O/fr Rest station with 21/O.R. etc. to 52 F.A. Handed over VADENCOURT Corps Stab'n station with 90 patients	
W.9.6.9.1 5.3.17			Headquarters 55 F.A. moved to W.9.6.9.1 Midland Huts. ALBERT Combined 40,000 Reported to A.D.M.S. Brown division remains forward under 54 F.A.	
"	6.3.17		Closed United R.33 central where working pieces F.A. are marching main dressing station.	
"	7.3.17		nil	
"	8.3.17		nil	
"	9.3.17		nil	
"	10.3.17		Instructed motor & horse transport evacuation from A.D.S at R.33 central returned. notice to assist at M.D.S. & Wounded	
"	11.3.17		nil	
"	12.3.17		Took over R.33 central as main dressing station. Two rows of F tents laced together to open on 13th inst Horses etc. remain at W.9.6 9.1.	

WAR DIARY or INTELLIGENCE SUMMARY

Army Form C. 2118

55 7.A. Vol 2 1

Place	Date	Hour	Summary of Events and Information	Remarks and references to Appendices
R 33 central	13.3.17		Opened M.D.S. at 12 noon. LENS 1000 / AMIENS 7000 / ALBERT Canal 1/2000	
"	14.3.17		Admitted/Wounded 3 off. 25 O.R. evac 3 off 22 O.R. 1 O.R. died 2 O.R. remaining. Cases very slow in arriving, on train in now beyond IRLES. S/Lt TRANTER awarded Military Medal, Pte THORNTON awarded Military Medal for military valour.	
"	15.3.17		Admitted 10 off 26 O.R. 10 off 23 O.R. to C.C.S. 5 remain	
"	16.3.17		Admitted 3 off (1 sick) 42 O.R. 2 off 38 O.R. to C.C.S. 7 remain	
"	17.3.17		Admitted 24 O.R. 27 to C.C.S. 4 remain	
"	18.3.17		Admitted 4 off 13 O.R. to C.C.S. 4 off 13 O.R. 3 remain. Capt JACKSON + one tent subdivision to MARLOY to take over Ops Rest station.	
"	19.3.17		Admitted 1 to C.C.S. 1 remain. Visited bearer Div IRLES. Pitched marquee at IRLES for M.D.S.	
"	20.3.17		1 remain. 1 go to duty, orders to be ready to close down at very short notice. Stretcher Bearers held complete extra divisions to No 3 C.C.S.	
"	21.3.17		Admitted 1 off 1 sick 4 wounded O.R. 15 sick 49 wounded all evacuated to C.C.S.	
"	22.3.17		Admitted 1 off 1 sick 3 wounded O.R. 14 sick 24 wounded all evacuated to C.C.S. Closed M.D.S. halted in town, marched to VADENCOURT	
VADENCOURT	23.3.17		Marched to SAVEUSE, reported arrival to Division at 55 9.B. Capt W.H. LISTER M.O. reported unit.	
SAVEUSE	24.3.17			

Army Form C. 2118

5574 Vol 2)
Mr Winder

WAR DIARY
or
INTELLIGENCE SUMMARY

FRANCE, 1:A. Sheet 2B. 1/40,000

AMIENS 1/100,000

HAZEBROUCK 1/100,000

(Erase heading not required.)

Place	Date	Hour	Summary of Events and Information	Remarks and references to Appendices
SAVEUSE In the train	26.3.17 26.3.17	7.20 p.m. 11 p.m.	Entrained at SALEUX 7.20 p.m. Arrived STEENBECQUE — marched to Billeting area BOESEGHEM — arrived 1.30 A.M. 27/3/17 no billets arranged — much difficulty in consequence	het Adjt ill. h.C.A. h.C.A.
BOESEGHEM	27.3.17		marched to Billets along new running N through I 3. d & b. Lt. Col. McWINDER DSO h Dir HA as ADMS.	
I 3 d + b	28.3.17		Hospital with accommodation for 30 cases of sick opened by Captain W.C. HARTGILL proceeded on leave to UK 29/3/17 to 8/4/17	W.H. sick.
"	29.3.17		Admitted 9 evacuated 4 Remain 5. 13 Reinforcements arrived taken on Strength	W.H.L
"	30.3.17		Admitted 3 Officers 11 O.R. evacuated 3 Officers 7 O.R. 9 O.R. remaining	W.H.L
"	31.3.17		Admitted 7 Quarantined 2 Remaining 14.	

140/1086

18th Div.

55th F.A.

COMMITTEE FOR THE
MEDICAL HISTORY OF THE WAR
Date -6 JUN.1917

B.E.F.

SUMMARY OF MEDICAL WAR DIARIES FOR 55th F.A. 18th Divn. 2nd Corps. 1st Army
7th Corps- 3rd Army from 29/4/17.

WESTERN FRONT. April- May. 1917.

O.C. Maj. M.G. Winder.

SUMMARISED UNDER THE FOLLOWING HEADINGS.

Phase "B" Battle of Arras- April- May. 1917.

1st Period Attack on Vimy Ridge April.

2nd Capture of Siegfried Line May.

B.E.F.

55th F.A. 18th Divn. 2nd Corps.   WESTERN FRONT.
O.C. Maj. M.G. Winder.   April. '17.
1st Army.
7th Corps- 3rd Army from 29/4/17.

Phase "B" Battle of Arras April- May. '17.
1st Period Attack on Vimy Ridge April.

1917.	Headquarters. At Boeseghen- 36a I.3.d & b.
April 3rd.	Weather: Accommodation: Very severe weather-snow and rain- Hospital premises were very bad with leaking roof.
20th.	Moves: To Lambres.
21st.	Moves: To Bethune.
27th.	Moves: To Pressy-Les-Pernes.
28th.	Moves: To Ficheux area- Tent Division took over M.D.S. from 96th Field Ambulance.
	Moves Detachment: 140 personnel to ARRAS.
29th.	Transfer. 7th Corps- 3rd Army.

B.E.F.

55th F.A. 18th Divn. 7th Corps. O.C. Maj. M.G. Winder. 3rd Army.

WESTERN FRONT.
April. '17.

Phase "B" Battle of Arras April- May. '17.
1st Period Attack on Vimy Ridge April.

1917.

April. 29th.   Transfer. 7th Corps- 3rd Army.

30th.   Medical Arrangements: M.D.S. at S.2.B. central contained a special abdominal Section with operating theatre and 5 Wards in Missen Huts for 40 cases.

Casualties. Totals for month.

Admissions 21 and 378.

Evacuations 19 and 308.

B.E.F.

<u>55th F.A. 18th Divn. 2nd Corps.</u>   <u>WESTERN FRONT.</u>
<u>O.C. Maj. M.G. Winder.</u>   <u>April. '17.</u>
<u>1st Army.</u>
<u>7th Corps- 3rd Army from 29/4/17.</u>

<u>Phase "B" Battle of Arras April- May. '17.</u>
<u>1st Period Attack on Vimy Ridge April.</u>

1917.	<u>Headquarters.</u> At Boeseghen- 36a I.3.d & b.
April 3rd.	<u>Weather: Accommodation:</u> Very severe weather-snow and rain- Hospital premises were very bad with leaking roof.
20th.	<u>Moves:</u> to Lambres.
21st.	<u>Moves:</u> To Bethune.
27th.	<u>Moves:</u> To Pressy-Les-Pernes.
28th.	<u>Moves:</u> To Ficheux area- Tent Division took over M.D.S. from 96th Field Ambulance.
	<u>Moves Detachment:</u> 140 personnel to ARRAS.
29th.	<u>Transfer.</u> 7th Corps- 3rd Army.

B.E.F.

55th F.A. 18th Divn. 7th Corps.   WESTERN FRONT.
O.C. Maj. M.G. Winder.   April. '17.
3rd Army.

Phase "B" Battle of Arras April- May. '17.
1st Period Attack on Vimy Ridge April.

1917.
April. 29th. Transfer. 7th Corps- 3rd Army.
30th. Medical Arrangements: M.D.S. at S.2.B. central contained
a special abdominal Section with operating theatre and
5 Wards in Missen Huts for 40 cases.
Casualties. Totals for month.
Admissions 21 and 378.
Evacuations 19 and 308.

WAR DIARY
or
INTELLIGENCE SUMMARY

Army Form C. 2118

Vol. 22

Winter 55 FA
W/H dide 9/22

HAZEBROUCK
FRANCE Sheet 36A

Place	Date	Hour	Summary of Events and Information	Remarks and references to Appendices
I3 d+b [BOESCHEM]	1.4.17		Admitted 10. Evacuated 1. To duty 2. Remaining 21	WH doyle
- do -	2.4.17		Admitted 13. Evacuated 4. To duty 2. Remaining 28	W.H.
- do -	3.4.17		Admitted 1 officer 13 O.R. Evacuated 1 officer 14 O.R. To duty 1. Remaining 26. Very snow weather - snow & rain - very bad - new Hospital marquee asked for from D.A.D.O.S. to replace Hospital tent	W.H.
- do -	4.4.17		Admitted 8. Evacuated 8. To duty 5. Remaining 21.	W.H.
- do -	5.4.17		Admitted 6. Evacuated 6. To duty 2. Remaining 18.	W.H.
- do -	6.4.17		Admitted 25. Evacuated 10. To duty 2. Remaining 31. Lieut J.L.D LEWIS R.A.M.C. T.C. Arrived from 39 General Hospital for duty and taken on strength this day.	W.H.
"	7.4.17		Admitted 10. Evacuated 11. 6 to duty. 24 remain	Apps
"	8.4.17		Admitted 14 off 11 O.R. evacuated 10 off 10 O.R. & CCS 9 to duty 16 remain	Apps
"	9.4.17		Admitted 13. T CCS. 9. 18 remain.	Apps
"	10.4.17		Admitted 1 off 7 O.R. evacuated 1 off 6 O.R. remain 18	Apps
"	11.4.17		Admitted 11 Evacuated 7 remain 20	Apps
"	12.4.17		Admitted 2 off 6 O.R. 2 off 5 O.R. evacuated remain 18	Apps
"	13.4.17		Admitted 4 off 22 O.R. evacuated 4 off 7 O.R. remain 31 Inspection by DDMS II and Corps	Apps
"	14.4.17		Admitted 7 evacuated 14 remain 15	Apps
"	15.4.17		Admitted 11 evacuated 6 remain 19	Apps
"	16.4.17		Admitted 8 evacuated 12 remain 19	Apps
"	17.4.17		Admitted 5 evacuated 4 remain 5	Apps
"	18.4.17		Admitted 1 off 12 O.R. evacuated 1 off 12 O.R. remain 16	Apps
"	19.4.17		Admitted 1 off 10 off 19 O.R. evacuated 1 off 29 O.R. Hospital closed ready to move	Apps
LAMBRES	20.4.17		Marched to LAMBRES with 55 I.B group. Admitted 14 evacuated 14	Apps

Army Form C. 2118
Vol 22

WAR DIARY
or
INTELLIGENCE SUMMARY
(Erase heading not required.)

Instructions regarding War Diaries and Intelligence Summaries are contained in F.S. Regs., Part II. and the Staff Manual respectively. Title Pages will be prepared in manuscript.

55 7A
M W Wander

HAZEBROUCK 1/100,000
LENS 1/100,000

Place	Date	Hour	Summary of Events and Information	Remarks and references to Appendices
BETHUNE	21.4.17		Marched to BETHUNE. Other Ranks 30 a more cases (up to 80) in building of civil hospital.	Appx
"	22.4.17		Admitted 2 off 8. O.R. evacuated 2 off. line of march.	Appx
"	23.4.17		2 admissions	Appx
"	24.4.17		21 admissions 6 evacuated 17 remain	Appx
"	25.4.17		4 admissions 2 evacuated 19 remain	Appx
"	26.4.17		1 off 4. O.R. admitted 1 off 6 O.R. evacuated 17 remain	Appx
"	27.4.17		9 admissions 4 evacuated 21 remain	Appx
"			16 th 11. O.R. admitted 1 off 24 O.R. evacuated 5 to Div (eventu (547A) 3 to duty. Closed & moved at 10.0 am to PRESSY LES PERNES. Returned animals to Rest & divisions.	Appx
PRESSY LES PERNES				
"	28.4.17		admitted 24 evacuated 24. Marched to FICHEUX area. Our 170 personnel who were entrained to ARRAS	Appx
S.2.B. vent	29.4.17		Spares and Francs 51.B.19. 40.000 Tent Division — 3 S.2.B. entered to take over M.D.S. from 96 7A. Became divisional N 20. e. 9.0. in reserve to be disposed of 54 7A	Appx
"	30.4.17		Completed taking over 9.0 am. M.D.S. contains a special abdominal section, with surgical team - Sister - theatre 9.5 wards (14 in each) with a conversation for 40 cases. Took over 3 off 140 R. from 96 7A. admitted 6 off 64 OR evacuated 6 off 59 OR 1 off 2. O.R. died. M.D.S. in for VIII Corps & for reception of officers & lying wounded only. Sick are not admitted. D.M.S. 3rd Army & S.S. Sir W. BABTIE visited M.D.S.	Appx

1875 Wt. W593/826 1,000,000 4/15 J.B.C. & A. A.D.S.S./Forms/C. 2118.

COMMITTEE FOR THE
MEDICAL HISTORY OF THE WAR
Date   10 JUL. 1917

No. 55. A.O.

1st Div

14/7/16

B.E.F.

SUMMARY OF MEDICAL WAR DIARIES FOR 55th F.A. 18th Divn. 2nd Corps. 1st Army 7th Corps- 3rd Army from 29/4/17.

WESTERN FRONT. April- May. 1917.

O.C. Maj. M.G. Winder.

SUMMARISED UNDER THE FOLLOWING HEADINGS.

Phase "B" Battle of Arras- April- May. 1917.

1st Period Attack on Vimy Ridge April.

2nd Capture of Siegfried Line May.

B.E.F.

55th F.A. 18th Divn. 7th Corps.   WESTERN FRONT.
O.C. Maj. M.G. Winder.   May. '17.
3rd Army.

Phase "B" Battle of Arras April- May. '17.
2nd Period Capture of Siegfried Line May.

1917.

May. 3rd. Operations. at 3.45 a.m. the whole Corps was engaged
           Casualties. wounded came in steadily from 7.30 a.m.
           Total admitted up to 10 a.m. = 6 and 94, 0 and 5 Died
           of wounds.

4th.   Casualties. Admitted 51 and 534, 0 and 27 died of
           wounds.
           Casualties R.A.M.C. 0 and 1 killed 0 and 2 wounded.

5th.   Casualties. Admitted 6 and 101 - 0 and 20 died of
           wounds.

6th.   Casualties. admitted 2 and 52- 0 and 7 died of
           wounds.
           Casualties R.A.M.C. 0 and 4 wounded.

10th.   Assistance. 100 attached Infantry used for general
           duties left to rejoin units.

17th.   Operations R.A.M.C. 0 and 80 daily working party
           assisted at 20th Casualty Clearing Station.

21st.   Operations. 33rd Division attacked.
           Casualties. admitted 11 and 170, 0 and 9 D of W.

22nd.   Casualties. Admitted 5 and 94 3 and 8 D. of W.

23rd.   Casualties. Admitted 31 and 31, 0 and 3 D. of W..

B.E.F.

<u>55th F.A. 18th Divn. 7th Corps.</u>   <u>WESTERN FRONT.</u>
<u>O.C. Maj. M.G. Winder.</u>   <u>May. '17.</u>
<u>3rd Army.</u>

<u>Phase "B" Battle of Arras April- May. '17.</u>
<u>2nd Period Capture of Siegfried Line May.</u>

1917.
May 31st.
cont.

<u>Casualties. Totals for month.</u> <u>Cont. from previous page.</u>

Admissions- 150- 1714.

Evacuations- 11% and 1539.

Died.   9 "   104.

B.E.F.

1.

55th F.A. 18th Divn. 7th Corps.　　WESTERN FRONT.
O.C. Maj. M.G. Winder.　　May. '17.
3rd Army.

Phase "B" Battle of Arras April- May. '17.
2nd Period Capture of Siegfried Line May.

1917.

May.3rd. Operations. at 3.45 a.m. the whole Corps was engaged
Casualties. wounded came in steadily from 7.30 a.m.
Total admitted up to 10 a.m. = 6 and 94, 0 and 5 Died
of wounds.

4th. Casualties. Admitted 51 and 534, 0 and 27 died of
wounds.
Casualties R.A.M.C. 0 and 1 killed 0 and 2 wounded.

5th. Casualties. Admitted 6 and 101 - 0 and 20 died of
wounds.

6th. Casualties. admitted 2 and 52- 0 and 7 died of
wounds.
Casualties R.A.M.C.   0 and 4 wounded.

10th. Assistance. 100 attached infantry used for general
duties left to rejoin units.

17th. OPerations R.A.M.C. 0 and 80 daily working party
assisted at 20th Casualty Clearing Station.

21st. Operations. 3grd Division attacked.
Casualties. admitted 11 and 170, 0 and 9 D of W.

22nd. Casualties. Admitted 5 and 94 3 and 8 D of W.

23rd. Casualties. Admitted 31 and 31, 0 and 3 D. of W..

B.E.F.

<u>55th F.A. 18th Divn. 7th Corps.</u>   <u>WESTERN FRONT.</u>
<u>O.C. Maj. M.G. Winder.</u>   <u>May. '17.</u>
<u>3rd Army.</u>

<u>Phase "B" Battle of Arras April- May. '17.</u>
<u>2nd Period Capture of Siegfried Line May.</u>

1917.
May 31st.
cont.

<u>Casualties.. Totals for month. cont.from previous page.</u>

Admissions- 150- 1714.

Evacuations- 112 and 1539.
Died.   9 "   104.

WAR DIARY or INTELLIGENCE SUMMARY

Army Form C. 2118

YK 23
5574
France 5.I.B LENS 1/100,000

Place	Date	Hour	Summary of Events and Information	Remarks and references to Appendices
S.2.B.central	1.5.17		admitted 20/fr 30.O.R. evacuated 10/fr 25 O.R. did 2o/fr 4.O.R. Capt G.A.BIRNIE.R.A.M.E T.C. admitted on 30/fr who to be taken on strength	appx
"	2.5.17		admitted 3 o/fr 40.O.R. evacuated 30/fr 35 O.R. did 10/fr 4.O.R.	appx
"	3.5.17		Fire at 3.45 a.m. which enfp engaged casualties coming in steadily from 7.30 am admitted 6o/fr 94.O.R. evacuated 6o/fr 86 O.R. did 5 O.R. this reports to 10.0 am when data was closed to make up totals. LT. J.I.D. LEWIS RAME T.C. posted to 7th Bn/fr in relief of Capt GATLEY. tonfranh attached who was wounded this morning. Sir A. BOWLRY Surgn visited S.G. MACPHERSON who arrested.	appx
"	4.5.17		admitted 51 o/fr 534 O.R. evac 49 o/fr 432 O.R. did 27.O.R. Capt BIRNIE posted No.9 C.C.S. 2 Swing to upper casualty. Capt W.L.HODGE R.A.M E T.C. reported & taken on strength. Pt. LUCAS T. No 40327 killed 3rd S/S TRANTER, wounded & executed. Pt. UNDERWOOD wounded on a Field Amb. S/S ELLIS. Pt. BULMER. Pt. FAIRLESS wounded remain at duty	appx
"	5.5.17		admitted 6o/fr 107.O.R. evacuated 9o/fr 134 O.R., 20 died. remain 2o/fr 46.O.R.	appx
"	6.5.17		admitted 20/fr 52.O.R. evacuated 20/fr 57.O.R. 7 died. Pte BIRKINSHAW. HOWE. NICHOLSON. PARTRIDGE Wounded, remain at duty	appx
"	7.5.17		admitted 3 officers & 27.O.R. evacuated 10/fr 26.O.R. 3 died. Pte THORNTON wounded V.C. bar to D.C.M S/S ELLIS D.C.M. L/Cpl RAINBOW " M.M. Pte PARTRIDGE " Dr.COX A.S & M.T. wounded/ M M	appx

Army Form C. 2118

WAR DIARY
or
INTELLIGENCE SUMMARY
(Erase heading not required.)

557A Vol 23

Place	Date	Hour	Summary of Events and Information	Remarks and references to Appendices
S.2 Bruts	8.5.17		admitted 8 off 25 O.R. evacuated 7 off 26 O.R. died 10 off 5 O.R. DMS & SS Sir W. DONOVAN visited	
"	9.5.17		admitted 3 off 19 O.R. evacuated 3 off 22 O.R. died 10 off 2 O.R.	
"	10.5.17		admitted 15 O.R. evacuated 1 off 13 O.R. died 3 O.R. all attached Monty 100 and for general duties left to rejoin units. Special surgical team 2 off 1 sister 1 PG left to rejoin the 20 C.C.S. for further stations on strength	
"	11.5.17		extra Lt RORIE F.M.R. A.M.C. S.R. reported for duty & taken on strength admitted 3 off 31 O.R. evacuated 2 off 55 O.R. died 1 off 6 O.R. Capt HODGE attd to 73rd Bde H.A.G. 1 tank off strength	
"	12.5.17		admitted 1 off 59 O.R. evacuated 1 off 49 O.R. died 8 O.R.	
"	13.5.17		admitted 18 evacuated 17 died 4	
"	14.5.17		admitted 2 off 43 O.R. evacuated 2 off 30 O.R. died 9	
"	15.5.17		admitted 2 off 26 O.R. evacuated 1 off 24 O.R. died 1 off 1 O.R.	
"	16.5.17		admitted 3 off 21 O.R. evacuated 1 off 17 O.R. died 1 off 4 O.R. Recurs diarrhoea rejoined headquarters	
"	17.5.17		admitted 1 off 30 O.R. evacuated 1 off 26 O.R. died 3 O.R. 80 O.R. slightly wounded with to await 20 C.C.S 1 Surgical team arrived from VI Corps units from	
"	18.5.17		20 C.C.S admitted 1 off 17 O.R. evacuated 1 off 21 O.R. died 4 O.R.	

WAR DIARY
INTELLIGENCE SUMMARY

Army Form C. 2118

5574 Vol 23

France 51.Q

Place	Date	Hour	Summary of Events and Information	Remarks and references to Appendices
S.2.B	19.5.17		Admitted 8. evacuated 6 died 1	
"	20.5.17		Admitted 10ff 56.O.R. evacuated 1 off 39.O.R. Died 10ff 7 O.R.	
"	21.5.17		83rd division attd. admitted all divisions 11 off 170.O.R. evacuated 10 off 161 O.R.	
"	22.5.17		died 9.O.R. Paid 3960 fr 25pp	
"			admitted 5 off 94 O.R. evacuated 3 off 87.O.R. Died 3 off 8.O.R. Capt W.H. LISTER RAMC evacuated sick	
"	23.5.17		admitted 31 off 31.O.R. evacuated 2 off 29 O.R. died 3.O.R.	
"	24.5.17		admitted 27. evacuated 16 died 7. Surgical team left to rejoin own unit 2nd Army under instructions from DMS. Third Army	
"	25.5.17		admitted 16 evacuated 12. died 7	
"	26.5.17		admitted 16 evacuated 23 died 1 Capt GT. LOUGHBOROUGH RAMC T.C. reported stolen on admitt.	
"	27.5.17		admitted 10 off 17 O.R. evacuated 10 ff 15 O.R. did 2	
"	28.5.17		admitted 19 O.R. evacuated 21. died 3.	
"	29.5.17		admitted 3 off 18 O.R. evacuated 3 off 11. O.R. died 6	
"	30.5.17		admitted 21 evacuated 15 died 1	
"	31.5.17		admitted 10ff 11.O.R. evacuated 1 off 9 O.R. under orders of DDMS. detached officers, sisters & O.R. rejoined personnel units today. Plan to continue	

140/2230

No 55 7.a.

June 1917

COMMITTEE FOR THE
MEDICAL HISTORY OF THE WAR
Date -7 AUG. 1917

Army Form C. 2118

WAR DIARY
or
INTELLIGENCE SUMMARY
(Erase heading not required.)

MMinden 5574 Vol 24

France 51B LENS 1/40,000 1/10,000 1/100,000

Place	Date	Hour	Summary of Events and Information	Remarks and references to Appendices
S.2.B.central	1.6.17		admitted 2 off, 11 O.R. evacuated 2 off, 10 O.R. died 1 O.R. Paid 197. Died pneumonia 2 SR 21st–31st. Started studying some magazines. admitted 1 to duty, 1 to ees. 2 to ees 11 remain	Antya
"	2.6.17		2 to ees 9 remain	Antya
"	3.6.17		admitted to off 5 O.R. evacuated 2 off 3 O.R. died 1 off	Antya
"	4.6.17		LT. A.J. O'LEARY rejoined for duty & taken on strength	Antya
"	5.6.17		evacuated 1 off 1 O.R. died 1 O.R. remain 9	
"	6.6.17		remaining 1 off R.A.M.C. & K.A. RICHARDS awarded M.E. Knee bitten horse to duty, 1 to ees. Remain	Antya
"	7.6.17		evacuated 22 died 5 remain 8	Antya
"	8.6.17		admitted 29 evacuated 22 died 5 remain 8	Antya
"	9.6.17		2 to duty 6 remain	Antya
"	10.6.17		6 remain. Left RAINBOW. Pte PARTRIDGE, Dr COX AT M?ASE Mebit Medal for 3.5.17 S.Sgt MITCHELL, S.Sgt VENESS mentioned in dispatches assault at CHERISY (being trained by him)	Antya
"	11.6.17		6 remain	Antya
"	12.6.17		1 to duty 5 remain	Antya
"	13.6.17		1 to ees 4 remain	Antya
"	14.6.17		4 to ees. Nil remain. Med. Store returned to ads in stores. Red Cross received.	Antya
"	15.6.17		moved to G.R.E.S.	Antya
"	16.6.17		closed. ditto	Antya
COIGNEUX	17.6.17		marched down during night to avoid heat. Also up to 20 Jn for brigade rich.	Antya
"	18.6.17		# S.Sgt ELLIS + Pte THORNTON awarded bars to D.C.M. action at CHERISY	Antya
"	19.6.17		admitted 1 off 4 O.R. 1 to ees. 1 off 3 O.R. remain	Antya
"	20.6.17		admitted 3. 1 off 2 O.R. to ees. 3 B e R skim. remain 1	Antya

Army Form C. 2118

WAR DIARY
or
INTELLIGENCE SUMMARY

(Erase heading not required.)

WW Winder   Vol 24

Place	Date	Hour	Summary of Events and Information	Remarks and references to Appendices
LOIGNEUX	21.6.17		Admitted 4 Remain 5	
"	22.6.17		Admitted 3 Evacuated 1 Remain 7	
"	23.6.17		Admitted 3 Evacuated 1 Capt. Rest Sta. 2 Remain 7 - Lt. Col. McKinder D.S.O. R.A.M.C. leave to U.K.	
"	24.6.17		Evacuated 2 Remain 5	
"	25.6.17		Admitted 5 Evacuated 2 Remain 8	
"	26.6.17		Remain 8	1 O.R. arrived as Reinforcements
"	27.6.17		Admitted 1 Remain 9	
"	28.6.17		Admitted 9 Evacuated 7 Capt. Rest Sta. 3 Remain 8	
"	29.6.17		Admitted 4 O.R. 1 Officer Evacuated 2 O.R. Remain 10/h. 10 O.R.	
"	30.6.17		Admitted 4 O.R. Evacuated 1 Off. 2 O.R. Capt. R.S. 3 Remain 9 - Received 55 Inf. Adv. Order No 118 with time table of move & settlement of Division to Fifth Army.	

LENS 1/100,000.
55 7A.

COMMITTEE FOR THE
MEDICAL HISTORY OF THE WAR
Date   10 SEP. 1917

No 55. 7. a.

Army Form C. 2118

WAR DIARY
or
INTELLIGENCE SUMMARY

(Erase heading not required.)

McMurdie for Menzies
55 Fld Amb. Vol. 25

Maps: LENS 1/100,000 BELGIUM & FRANCE Sheet 28
HAZEBROUCK 1/100,000

Place	Date	Hour	Summary of Events and Information	Remarks and references to Appendices
COLGNEUX	1.7.16		Admitted 3 Evacuated 3 C.R.S. 1 Remain 8	R.A.
"	2.7.16		Admitted 16th. 15 O.R. Evacuated 16th. 11 O.R. C.R.S. 12 O.R. Remain NIL	R.A.
CAUMESNIL	3.7.16		Closed & marched to CAUMESNIL. Brigade closing in DOULLENS for entrainment. Nil admitted Ambce sitting	R.A.
WIPPENHOEKE	4.7.16		Admitted 13 Evacuated 13 Entrained DOULLENS for HOPOUTRE (near POPERINGHE)	R.A.
"	5.7.16		Billeted in WIPPENHOEKE area Resting admitted 6 evacuated 1 to C.C.S. 5 to D.R.S.	
H27d4.1.	6.7.16		Took over from 96 F.A. an ambulance Headquarters & C.M.D.S. at H27d4.1 also C.M.D.S. ¼ mile N.W. H27.C.1.9. which is under construction consisting of series of Alt marquees single lined in series of 3" & 2 large "3"-inch Miner huts. Took over A.D.S. WOODCOTE HOUSE 1.26.e.4.2. with collecting posts at BUND. 1.21.a.9.9. and COW FARM. 1.22.B.8.4. Personnel WOODCOTE HOUSE. 2 Offrs 2 nco 16 pt 1 another Ford 1 motor cycle " BUND 1 Offr 1 " 14 pts " COW FARM. 1 " 4 pts 4 pts with 8 men detached to R.A.P. C.M.D.S. on completion will be occupied but Huns + A. were shelled out when they tried to open it. Wounded received from 18th Division and from division on left ie 8th Division. Trade & dies a Right ie 23rd Division in. Open from 12 noon.	Info

WAR DIARY
or
INTELLIGENCE SUMMARY

Army Form C. 2118

HMWinter
A/M
55 FA

Halfbrayer
Beginning of issue 28 / 100,000
100,000

Place	Date	Hour	Summary of Events and Information	Remarks and references to Appendices
H27d4.1	7.7.17		admitted 2 off 42 O.R. T.ees 2 off 31 O.R. died 11. D.R. @ BEARDSLEY MT A 5e 557A wounded evacuated	Appx
"	8.7.17		admitted 2 off 115 O.R. evacuated 20 off 107 O.R. died 2 O.R. duty 6 O.R. Visited A.D.S. WOODCOTE Horse Pond obstacle. Concrete & sandbags for about 50 cases. BUND. Two dug outs holding about 30 cases. Part of Courthouse in use as advanced post is not suitable or sufficiently protected to store cases. Roads near A.D.S. bad. Shelled all around SHRAPNEL CORNER. Can use (advanced) road a little north of this corner. DDMS inspected	Appx Appx
"	9.7.17		admitted 5 off 28 O.R. evac 5 off 24 O.R. 3 to 54 FA (9) remain 1	Appx
"	10.7.17		admitted 26 evacuated 21 died 2 duty 1 remain 3. Took ADMS around Adv dressing station & Collecting posts.	Appx
"	11.7.17		admitted 1 off 62 O.R. evac 1 off 58 O.R. remain 7	Appx
"	12.7.17		admitted 1 off 64 O.R. evac 1 off 63 O.R. died 4 duty 4	Appx Appx
"	13.7.17		admitted 2 off 58 O.R. evac 2 off 46 O.R. duty 7 remain 5 Antirabies hosp staff in	Appx Appx
"	14.7.17		admitted 3 off 81 O.R. evac 3 off 64 O.R. died 12 duty 2 remain 8	Appx
"	15.7.17		admitted 7 off 83 O.R. evac 4 off 65 O.R. evac 4 off to 54 FA (9 cases) 20 off 20 O.R. duty 1 off 10 R. duty 14 off	Appx
"	16.7.17		admitted 6 off 95 O.R. evac 5 off 71 O.R. died 3 O.R. duty 1 off 10 R. remain 7 O.R. with ADS at 27.C.1.9 opened at 12 noon	Appx
H27e.1.9	17.7.17		admitted 2 off 86 O.R. evac 1 off 56 O.R. died 4 O.R. to 54 FA 10 off 17 O.R. (Bm) remain 16 O.R.	Appx
"	18.7.17		admitted 2 off 75 O.R. evac 2 off 71 O.R. died 2 O.R. to 54 FA 3 O.R. duty 2 remain 13	Appx

WAR DIARY
or
INTELLIGENCE SUMMARY

(Erase heading not required.)

Army Form C. 2118

M Winder
5537 Vol 25

MAPS. HAZEBROUCK 1/100,000 Sheet 28 1/10,000

Place	Date	Hour	Summary of Events and Information	Remarks and references to Appendices
H27.c.1.9	19/7/17		Admitted 4 off 115 O.R. Evac 4 off 81 O.R. to 54 F.A. 210 R. died 4 duty 3 remain 19	appx
"	20/7/17		Admitted 4 off 93 O.R. Evac 3 off 70 O.R. to 54 F.A. 1 off 5 O.R. died 6 duty 10. Remain 21	appx
"	21/7/17		pointed A.D.S. C.P. Admitted 4 off 97 O.R. Evac 3 off 77 O.R. to 54 F.A. 3 O.R. died 4 duty 17 O.R. remain 33 O.R. Advance party 96 F.A. arrived to take over C.M.D.S.	appx
"	22/7/17		Admitted 5 off 89 O.R. Evac 1 off 64 O.R. (8 cases) died 1 off 9 O.R. duty 15 remain 1 & 26	appx
"	23/7/17		Admitted 5 off 200 O.R. to C.C.S. & 2 to 54 F.A. 5 off 111 O.R. died 7 to duty 1 off 16 O.R. remain 10 Conf. held on afternoon of 23rd. 1 M.A.C. driver wounded no other casualties	appx
"	24/7/17		Admitted 4 off 118 O.R. Evac 4 off 79 O.R. 54 F.A. 240 duty 9 duty 7 to 96 F.A. 9. moved Hqrs to H 27.d.4.1.9 Rd. over C.M.D.S. to 96 F.A. LT O'LEARY to 19 ccs. today situated at DICKEBUSCH	appx
OUDERDOM	25/7/17		moved to OUDERDOM evening of 24th No accommodation available for temporary duty Closed. Transport remainder of RENINGHELST. I tent sub division	appx
"	26/7/17		closed	appx
"	27/7/17		" LT O'LEARY reported for duty from 19 ccs. & taken on strength	appx
"	28/7/17		closed	appx
"	29/7/17			
"	30/7/17		Division in support of 30th Division with 24th Division on the right. 8th supported by 25th on the left. After 30th Div attack has succeeded 18th Div attack with 53rd Bde starting J.8.c.b.14 - J.14.c.2.3 (Black line) & J.3.d.5.0 - J.9.d.2.0 green line being their objective. 56 F.A. leaves clean 53 F.B. cases being taken over from them by 55 F.A. becomes carries to ZILLEBEKE thence by car to A.D.S. WOODCOTE HOUSE 54 F.A. to establish a Collecting Post in J.13. and a. 56 F.A. to establish a car point also horsible on the MENIN Road. When they place no ambulance of evacuation except for walking wounded to permitted on MENIN Road. 30th = 4 day	

Army Form C. 2118

WAR DIARY
or
INTELLIGENCE SUMMARY
(Erase heading not required.)

WW later 557.A. - WA25
BELGIUM + FRANCE
Sheet 28

Place	Date	Hour	Summary of Events and Information	Remarks and references to Appendices
H.27.d.4.1.	31-7-17		Transport etc. left at Headquarters. Bearer Division moved up at 5.30 am together with Headquarters other than Transport & details. Advanced Headquarters Cow Farm ZILLEBEKE. Bearer division moved up to following 33 Inf Bde to Black Line for clearing from the attack. Held up about 1st objective of 30th division who had not taken the Black line. 56 & 55 7.A. Bearer divisions made head quarters at west end of tunnel MENIN Rd. & cleared continuously by relays to ZILLEBEKE where cars were put on horse & motor ambulances. Clearing to adv dressing station WOODCOTE HOUSE. 53.9.3. withdrawn during evening of 31.7. Wounded 55 7.A. to c/c TAYLOR H. TOTHILL. L/Cpl BULMER. Pte RICHARDSON. KIRBYSON. VALE evacuated. Pte WILLINSCROFT to DRS (547A) Pte NICHOLLS. H. admitted & duck to duty. Pte THORNTON. MULLIN. WOLSTENCROFT. SMART. Sgt JONES wounded & remain at duty.	Appx/10

140/2264

No. 55. T.A.

Aug. 1917

COMMITTEE FOR THE
MEDICAL HISTORY OF THE WAR
Date -1 OCT. 1917

10

55-7A Aust. Army Form C. 2118

55-7A Aust FM Vol 26

WAR DIARY
INTELLIGENCE SUMMARY
(Erase heading not required.)

M.F. Finder
Belgium & France Sheet 28
HAZEBROUCK 1/100,000

Place	Date	Hour	Summary of Events and Information	Remarks and references to Appendices
H27.d.4.1.	1.8.17		Received orders to withdraw from ZILLEBEKE as soon as 18th Div Casualties were clear. At 5.0 am bearers went up to tunnel MENIN Road & cleared cases. Very heavy Rain and the enemy extremely bad. Ordered 567A bearers back to own unit & RAME Horse & Motor Ambulance to rejoin unit. Settled down "squads in billets. ZILLEBEKE & Cow Farm handed over to 30th Div 7.A. all 18th Div back to H27.d.4.1. by 11.0 am. Reported personally to A.D.M.S.	
"	2.8.17		Recommended S.Sgt Taylor, Pte Perry & Walmsley for Military Medal	
WARATAH G15.a.3.0	3.8.17		Took over 11th Div Rest Station from 547A. Patients 5 off. 186 O.R. Began Division union DICKEBUSCH. 1 tent subdivision union at 100 e5	
"	4.8.17		10/11 9 or to CES 21 t.o. 5 8 off. 204 O.R. remain. Orders to hand over to 57 A Motor 5th & take over II nd C.M.D.S. at H.27.e.19. the same day.	
H27.e.19	5.8.17 (6.8.17)		Handed over Div rest to 567A. Marched to II nd C.M.D.S. Recording from midday 5.8.17 till completed taking over at 12 noon. All mil & wounded of II nd Corps received from officer with clerks from respective divisions admitted wounded S.W. & walking (8th Div in contact of latter) 8 off. 350 O.R. Mt Lister, M.C. Pte Ower wounded & Cpl Ranie wounded remain dead.	
"	7.8.17		557A bearer div relieved 54 in the Line. Admitted Sevère a night 110 off 374 O.R.	

WAR DIARY
or
INTELLIGENCE SUMMARY

Army Form C. 2118

(Erase heading not required.)

M.M. Winter 55744 . Vol 26

Map HAZEBROUCK Belgium & France sheet 28 1/100,000 / 1/40,000

Place	Date	Hour	Summary of Events and Information	Remarks and references to Appendices
H27c1.9.	9/8/17		Tent addirimsson 56th Div refitted for duty. Tent addirimson 5574 rejoined from hostices. Light Service waggon admitted 18 o/r 237 O.R. Tent addirimson 5574 rejoined new cament. Establishment new cament 1 Tent Div 5574	
"	9/8/17		2 tent subs 24 " " 2 " " 26 " " 2 " " 56 " " +79 extra any men for bearers	
"	10.8.17		admitted 110 o/r 342 O.R. 18th & 24th divisions attached admitted 110 o/r 416 O.R. wounded	
"	11.8.17		admitted 32 o/r 1003 O.R. wounded admitted 28 o/r 626 O.R. wounded. Reserve division rejoined & remain in reserve	
"	12.8.17			
"	13.8.17		admitted 14 o/r 353 O.R. Consulting surgeon 5th army visited	
"	14.8.17		admitted 13 o/r 263 O.R. wounded	
"	15.8.17		admitted 11 o/r 404 O.R. " British aeroplane down in lines enemy dead 4 men wounded & evacuated 1 remains at duty. Beaver Div. up to Woodcote House	
"	16.8.17		admitted wounded 32 o/r 777 O.R.	
"	17.8.17		admitted wounded 71 o/r 2186 O.R. Beaver division rejoined from Woodcote House	
"	18.8.17		admitted wounded 25 o/r 462 O.R. Rounded over II and Corps M.D.S. to 42nd F.A.	

1/4th Div

WAR DIARY
or
INTELLIGENCE SUMMARY
(Erase heading not required.)

Army Form C. 2118

M/Winter 55TA A.A. Vol 26

HAZEBROUCK 1/100,000

Place	Date	Hour	Summary of Events and Information	Remarks and references to Appendices
BLANKAART	19.8.17		Personnel by lorries, transport by road, billeted in farm, accommodation for 20 patients.	copies
ZEGGERS CAPPEL	20.8.17		Sgt Taylor, Pte Perry & Wheatley awarded Military Medal	copies
"	21.8.17		Nil	copies
"	22.8.17		6 admission 6 remain	copies
"	23.8.17		2 admission 2 to ccs 6 remain	copies
"	24.8.17		2 admission 1 to duty 7 remain	copies
"	25.8.17		3 admission 3 to ccs 1 to duty 6 remain	copies
"	26.8.17		4 admission 4 to ccs 2 to duty 4 remain	copies
"	27.8.17		3 admission 7 remain	copies
"	28.8.17		1 O/R 2.O.R. admission 1 O/R to ccs 1 O.R. to duty 8 remain	copies
"	29.8.17		2 admission 1 to ccs 9 remain	copies
"	30.8.17		2 admission 3 to ccs 3 to duty 5 remain	copies
"	31.8.17		1 O/R 1.O.R. admission 6 remain	copies
"			3 admission 1 O/R 3.O.R. to ccs 1 duty 5 remain	copies

No. 55 7.O.

COMMITTEE FOR THE
MEDICAL HISTORY OF THE WAR
Date -5 NOV.1917

WAR DIARY or INTELLIGENCE SUMMARY

Army Form C. 2118

55 2/n Auf
M/Winden Vol 27
557A

Place	Date	Hour	Summary of Events and Information	Remarks and references to Appendices
BLANKART from NEU ZEGGERS CAPPEL	1.9.17		admitted 5 remain 10	
"	2.9.17		admitted 10/f 4 O.R. evacuated 10/f 1.a.R. duty 1, remain 12	
"	3.9.17		admitted 6. evacuated 2 duty 4; remain 12	
"	4.9.17		admitted 3 evacuated 1 remain 14	
"	5.9.17		admitted nil evacuated 2 duty 2 remain 10	
"	6.9.17		admitted 1 duty 2 remain 9	
"	7.9.17		admitted 1 duty 1 remain 8	
"	8.9.17		admitted 5 evacuated 3 duty 3 remain 7, Lt O'LEARY evacuated hysteria	
"	9.9.17		admitted 2 O/f 3.O.R. evacuated 2 O/f 2.O.R. duty 1 remain 7 Capt APPLEYARD W. RAMC. T. arrived 9.9.17	
"	10.9.17		admitted 2 evacuated 1 duty 1 remain 7 & taken on strength	
"	11.9.17		Lt PARSONS. I.T. U.S.M.O R.E. reported for duty 10th & taken on strength. Lt RORIE S.R. posted to Rouen Depôt & struck off admitted 2 evacuated 1 remain 8.	
"	12.9.17		strength (S. 12th in lieu) admitted 5 evacuated 1 remain 12	
"	13.9.17		admitted 4 evacuated 5 duty 2 remain 9	
"	14.9.17		admitted 3 evacuated 2 duty 2 remain 8	
"	15.9.17		admitted 1 remain 9	
"	16.9.17		admitted 3 evacuated 5 duty 1 remain 6 Capt APPLEYARD both to 47 ces & struck off strength Capt W.B.DAVY RAMC-T.F. posted to 2/A from 47 ces taken on strength	
"	17.9.17		admitted 1 duty 2 remain 5	
"	18.9.17		admitted 7 evacuated 2 duty 2 remain 8	
"	19.9.17		admitted 2 evacuated 2 remain 8	
"	20.9.17		admitted 2 evacuated 1 remain 8	
"	21.9.17		admitted 4 evacuated 4 duty 2 remain 6	
"	22.9.17		admitted 4 evacuated 1 O/f Care el stal 1 O/f 3.O.R. remain 4. After admissions 4 P.O.S.O. closed	

WAR DIARY
or
INTELLIGENCE SUMMARY
(Erase heading not required.)

Army Form C. 2118

557A Vol 27

M Winter

HAZEBROUCK. 1/80,000
Sheets 27 & 28 BELGIUM & FRANCE 1/40,000

Place	Date	Hour	Summary of Events and Information	Remarks and references to Appendices
Sheet 27.9.29.d 5.9 L'EBBE. Farm	23.9.17		Personnel by train, transport by road, arrived 2.0 pm. reported to D.D.M.S. XVIII corps. Detailed 2 tent subdivisions to CHATEAU ROUGE, Sheet 28 G.2.a.2.4. Orders to take over from the Rest station and Corps Sick Collecting Station at Chateau Rouge on 24th inst with 2 tent subdivisions, blanket store B/107 L.EBBE farm with one tent subdivision	Appx
"	24.9.17		taking over above stations	Appx
"	25.9.17		Reported completion taking over stations. Cases are all received in batches of @ 12 stretcher cases on Hazebrouck lorries. Hutments being provided	Appx Appx
"	26.9.17		nil	Appx
"	27.9.17		nil	Appx
"	28.9.17		nil	
G.2.a.2.4 Sheet 28	29.9.17		moved Hy. 7A to Chateau Rouge. Present distribution Hy. + 2 tent subdivisions at Chateau Rouge. 1 tent subdivision & bearer division at L'EBBE farm; transport, officers mess and 1 invalid Road N of POPERINGHE.	Appx
"	30.9.17		Bombing raid on POPERINGHE 9.30 pm 29 to 2.30 am 30th 50 Casualties with 11 deaths brought in. dressed and sent on to C.C.S. REMY more cases picked up in own station direct.	Appx
			local funerals will be patients 14.40 pm	

No. 55. 7 0.

COMMITTEE FOR THE
MEDICAL HISTORY OF THE WAR
Date -8 DEC. 1917

WAR DIARY or INTELLIGENCE SUMMARY

(Erase heading not required.)

Army Form C. 2118

No 16 Vol 28

M.M.Winter
5574

Maps Hazebrouck 1:100,000
Sheets 27 & 28 BELGIUM & FRANCE 1:40,000

Place	Date	Hour	Summary of Events and Information	Remarks and references to Appendices
G.20.a.2.4. Sheet 28	1/10/17		Bombing raid slight last night no casualties reported. Fatigue party 30th Sept & later with strength.	AdjR/o
"	2/10/17		Dr. Powditch S.A.S.C. 4T. killed by aircraft fragment of shell. Crowds of inch posted out to E.S. & R.C.S.	AdjR/o
"	3/10/17		nil	AdjR/o
"	4/10/17		nil	AdjR/o
"	5/10/17		nil	AdjR/o
"	6/10/17		nil	AdjR/o
"	7/10/17		nil	AdjR/o
"	8/10/17		nil ... Pte 16807 Reed machine miller	AdjR/o
"	9/10/17		nil ... Capt ASHMORE R.A.M.C. posted to 8th R.Sussex	AdjR/o
"	10/10/17		Between attack off attack. Lt & two TURNER posted to Kt 18 General Hosp posted for duty & struck off strength. Large numbers of shells but a hand but passed through tent subdivision posted to W.W.E. Post Sheet 28. H.3.d.5.8. Beaver division ordered to 151.Y farm Sheet 28 B 29.d.8.8. to report to O.C. 56TH under where division they will work.	AdjR/o
"	11/10/17		nil	AdjR/o
"	12/10/17		559 B. attached at POELCAPPELLE 55 7A between cleaning wounded. Became casualties killed Pte SHEPHERD. NEALE. WINTERBOTTOM 17. Wounded Pte KEY DOUGLAS. BAYNHAM. MULLAN. GIBBINS. FULLER CARNEY. READ. A.T. HAGGIS. all evacuated Pte WALLIS A. remain at duty.	AdjR/o
"	13/10/17		Beaver division rejoined hdqrs.	AdjR/o
"	14/10/17		Pte 16.80.7 Reed machine miller	AdjR/o
"	15/10/17		nil	AdjR/o

WAR DIARY
or
INTELLIGENCE SUMMARY

(Erase heading not required.)

Army Form C. 2118

M/Winter 557A Vol 28

HAZEBROUCK Sheets 27 & 28 BELGIUM & FRANCE

Place	Date	Hour	Summary of Events and Information	Remarks and references to Appendices
G 2 a 2.4 Sheet 28	16.10.17		Bearer division 557A moved up in reserve to 567A	Appx
"	17.10.17	11:42am	Lt SENIOR, E.H. RAME (R.A.S.C.) joined for duty crowds of patients rated to E/S a ERS	Appx
"	18.10.17		nil	Appx
"	19.10.17		nil	Appx
"	20.10.17		nil	Appx
"	21.10.17		nil	Appx
"	22.10.17		Col 16.30 Head of bearer division completed 557A bearer division posted 567A for duty. Others on stay at 18th Division attached POELCAPPELLE Capture of intelligence. Capt HALLINAN RAMC S wounded in action 2nd evacuating wounded	Appx
"	23.10.17		Sgt ELLIS & Pte PRICE A.J. killed in action 2nd Wounded & evacuated Ptes GARVEY, WHARTON, McKAIN, THOMPSON A, WILSON M, Cpl HEAP P, Ptes SNEFFINGTON, THORNTON, WOOD R, BRADSHAW, WELCH, WILSON M, Cpl HEAP P, Pte BURNETT, HUGHES, NOCK, SMITH E, Ptes GUTHRIE, ALTON. Bearer division rejoined Hy on night of 22nd	Appx
"	24.10.17		Test subdivision rejoined Hy from Corps W.W.C.P. nil	Appx
"	25.10.17		Capt T.W. JACKSON posted M.O. 2 Survey Bty from 23.d G.O.C. visited a congratulated the bearers on their work.	Appx
"	26.10.17		nil	Appx
"	27.10.17		nil	Appx
"	28.10.17		nil	Appx
"	29.10.17		7A 32d Divreme received totals ans XVIII info ORS, OSCS + ships depot	Appx
"	30.10.17		POPERINGHE shelled from 11:0pm 30th that 30RH several in neighbourhood Pte WALMSLEY had chest gland scapula evacuated. Two HAC came damaged of 7A on fill in yard completed handing over to 32nd Div receiving certificate from evacuation.	Appx
"	31.10.17		marched to PORTSEA camp sheet 27 7.1.6.4.2 refuted arrived. Evidence survey closed. Paid 24 h. bonus purchase rail to 31/17	Appx

140/2578

No. 55. 7.0.

COMMITTEE FOR
MEDICAL HISTORY
Date 17 JAN 1918

WAR DIARY or INTELLIGENCE SUMMARY

Army Form C. 2118

55- Fd Amb Vol 29
Lt W Wynder 55 F.A.

MAPS. HAZEBROUCK 1/100,000 Belgium & N.W. France sheets 27, 28, 20. Sheet 20 S.W.4 BIXSCHOOTE 1/10,000

Place	Date	Hour	Summary of Events and Information	Remarks and references to Appendices
Sheet 27 7 A 4.2	1.11.17		LT. PARSONS U.S.M.O.R.P. proceeded for temporary duty with 18th D.A.C PORTSEA Camp 7.6.4.c. in about 1 mile from PROVEN.	Appx
"	2.11.17		LT. PARSONS posted permanently to 18th D.A.C.	Appx
"	3.11.17		ADS 50.O.R. sent forward to take over line from 35th Div. F.A. to RCS2 to CRS 2 one officer admitted to.	Appx
B10 c.3.3.	4.11.17		7A moved up to BLEUET farm Hy of 7A sheet 28. B10 c 3.3 ADS. 1 M.O. 1 nursing Orderly H.Q. 2 orderlies 3 squads evacuation ste. at GREEN M.DD sheet 20 U25 c.10.2. tellet-post 2 N.C.O. 1 nursing H.O. 2 orderlies 3 squads at RUISSEAU farm sheet 20 U 21 c 9.1. Relay post NEY wood (1 N.C.O. 10 men) U11 c 4.6. a NEY x roads (1 N.C.O. 6 men) U16 d 6.6. Relay post VEE Road (1 N.C.O. 2 wards) V11 d 2.6. R.A.P. LOUVOIS farm U11 a 9.4. & EGYPT House U12 d 2.9. one squad at each R.A.P. EGYPT Home not established till night 6/11/17 Cases brought down by bearers along duck boarding to NEY farm. thence by tram from here by Decauville line to EMDS sheet 28. B 22 b. 8.4. @ EWWP at to GREEN MILL B17 d 8.8. Horse lines less Horse and wagon 2 limber 2 water cart arr at Sheet 28 B A 4 central	
"	5.11.17		Visited A.D.S. Sgt Pauls, Pte Andrew, BROWN E.W.C. BURNETT. HAZELWOOD L ELLIOTT NEWMAN. E.W. SILLS. TILLEY. WILKINSON. WILLIAMS D. WINTERBOTTOM A.H. gon to Shed a all evacuated	Appx
"	6.11.17		LT LEITH R.G. U.S.M.O. R.E. joined for duty 5th	Appx
"	7.11.17		Cpl NEAL. Pte FOWLER. HUGHES JOHNSON. C. LAWES. MORBEY. THOMPSON GR. G. BROWN, all evacuated Visited ADS & collecting post RUISSEAU farm Pte NURSE, MARRON & EMBRY gassed all evacuated	Appx

WAR DIARY
or
INTELLIGENCE SUMMARY

Army Form C. 2118

Vol 29

MW Winder
55 FA

MAPS HAZEBROUCK 100,000 BELGIUM & FRANCE 20, 27, 28 40,000 / 10,000
Sheet 28 S.W. 4 BIXSCHOOTE (POELCAPPELLE OCTP.)

Place	Date	Hour	Summary of Events and Information	Remarks and references to Appendices
B/C 83 Hut 28	8·11·17		10/A 6 a.m. rate of 56 FA relieved 55 FA at forward posts	ditto
"	9·11·17		Relief of forward posts by 56 FA completed GREEN MILL A.D.S. set remains staffed by 55 FA	ditto
"	10·11·17		27 reinforcements arrived	ditto
"	11·11·17		nil	ditto
"	12·11·17		nil	ditto
"	13·11·17		1/A 6 a.m. rate of 54 FA relieved 56 FA at forward posts	ditto
"	14·11·17		Relief of forward posts by 54 FA completed	ditto
"	15·11·17		nil	ditto
"	16·11·17		nil	ditto
"	17·11·17		10 reinforcements arrived & taken on strength	ditto
"	18·11·17		Relieved 6 a.m. rate of 54 FA at forward posts	ditto
"	19·11·17		Completed relief of forward area with 55 FA 2nd division	ditto
"	20·11·17		nil	ditto
"	21·11·17		nil	ditto
"	22·11·17		Lt. H. TRIM heart history model L.H. AMEY, Pt. HALL, A. HARRADINE, HUGHES T. Milton half to (POELCAPPELLE OCTP.)	ditto
"	23·11·17		Visited CRONNE farm U 15 d. there is an adjacent hill from which if increased by a tunnel dugout behind it would be suitable for an A.D.S. or collecting post & more convenient than RUISSEAU farm	ditto
"	24·11·17		10 reinforcements arrived & taken on strength	ditto
"	25·11·17		56 FA 2nd division relieved 55 in forward area	ditto
"	26·11·17		Lt. KING B. & Lt. NAFEY H.W. M.O. R.S. U.S.A. joined for duty	ditto
"	27·11·17		Capt. A.E. HALLINAN posted to 7 & Z Kent returned off strength	ditto

Army Form C. 2118

WAR DIARY
or
INTELLIGENCE SUMMARY
(Erase heading not required.)

M/Winter
557A Vol 29

Maps, Belgium & France Sheets 20.28 & 36

Place	Date	Hour	Summary of Events and Information	Remarks and references to Appendices
B10.c 3.3. Sheet 28	28.11.17	nil		Appx
"	29.11.17	nil		Appx
"	30.11.17		Handed over post at RUISSEAU Farm to R.F.A. in exchange for a large hill dug out at CRAONNE Farm. U.15.d.4.5. Also opened a relay post to SIGNAL Farm U 21 c 2.0.	Appx

COMMITTEE FOR THE
MEDICAL HISTORY OF THE WAR
Date −1 FEB. 1918

WAR DIARY or INTELLIGENCE SUMMARY

Army Form C. 2118

55th Fd Amb
MM winda 557A
Vol 30

HAZEBROUCK 1/40,000
Belgium & France Sheet 20.28 1/40,000 Sheet 28 S.W. 4 1/10,000

Place	Date	Hour	Summary of Events and Information	Remarks and references to Appendices
BIOC 3.3. Sheet 28	1-12-17		An elephant hutch is being erected behind new post at CRAONNE Farm to accommodate stretcher cases	Appx
"	2-12-17		nil	Appx
"	3-12-17		nil	Appx
"	4-12-17		Lt Col. M.A. WINDER, D.S.O. proceeded on leave 5/12 – 5/11	Lt Col. hautspill
"	5-12-17		Frosty weather	K.A.
"	6-12-17		"	K.A.
"	7-12-17		nil	K.A.
"	8-12-17		Bearer Divs 66 Fd. Amb. relieved Bearer Divs 34 Fd. Amb. in the line	K.A.
"	9-12-17		Nil	K.A.
"	10-12-17		Nil	K.A.
"	11-12-17		Visited CRAONNE FARM – New dressing station complete – capable of holding 9 stretcher cases Cork house not completed. Also visited GRUYTERZALE FARM – site of proposed ADP Bearer Posts Cork house at CRAONNE Farm now completed. Tram line and necker road to	K.B.
"	12-12-17		No work in this connection appears to be contemplated.	LEE BEND?
"			Nil	K.A.
"	13-12-17		Shared ADMS 57th Div. round forward area and lines of evacuation.	K.A.
"	14-12-17		Shared OC Julienne Fd. Amb. and SADMS 57th Div. round forward area and lines of evacuation.	K.A.
"	15-12-17		Capt. Richards with 60 O.R. & Subalterns proceeded to run new NORDAUSQUES as Advanced Billeting Party	K.A.
"	16-12-17		2 Officers 30 O.R. wired from 2/2 Eversea Fd. Amb.	K.A.
MONNECOVE	17-12-17		Remainder 1/2 bearer Fd. Amb. wired & took over HA at BLUET Farm – also Adv. Dress Stat GREEN MILLS Transport marched by road to ZEGGERS CAPPEL to NORDAUSQUES run – Billet in MONNECOVE. Reminder Personnel by Bearer in tr line by train to MONNECOVE	K.A.
"	18-12-17		Transport by road from ZEGGERS CAPPEL to MONNECOVE and marched to billets in MONNECOVE. Bearers from the line by car to MONNECOVE. Whole Unit stats for sick from Brigade Area.	K.A.

1875 Wt. W593/826 1,000,000 4/15 J.B.C. & A. A.D.S.S./Forms/C.2118.

WAR DIARY or INTELLIGENCE SUMMARY

Army Form C. 2118

BELGIUM - FRANCE Sheet 19
HAZEBROUCK 5A. 1/100,000
55 Fd. Amb.

Place	Date	Hour	Summary of Events and Information	Remarks and references to Appendices
MONNECOVE	19.12.17		Visited Forest of TOURNEHEM area to make Medical arrangements for Army units engaged in Lumber work. Total personnel 1245 in the various camps including P.O.W. Coy and Chinese Lab. Coy. Established 1st Aid Post at the Sawmill near the Ford between BONNINGUES and TOURNEHEM – with a L/Cpl. (Nursing Section) permanently on duty there. M.O. with all camps daily by car.	K.H.
"	20.12.17		Received return last night to take over GRENOGE Farm Rest Station (RTR Corps) with a tentsub division. Capt. Richardson with Adv. party 16 O.R. proceeded to day. Situation 2 tray between LEDERZELE & MILLAM. Inspected the place & found it had been used as Skin depot – hurt by the patients being Scabies and Impetigo. No efficient means of disinfestation so applied for Clayton disinfestor	K.H.
"	21.12.17		Lt. Knig MRC USA with remainder personnel of Tent Sub div completed taking over GRENOGE FARM Admitted 2 Remain 3	K.H.
"	22.12.17		Admitted 1 Evac. 1 Remain 3 – very hard frost	K.H.
"	23.12.17		Admitted 3 Evac. 2 Remain 4 "	K.H.
"	24.12.17		Admitted 4 Evac. 2 Death 1 Remain 5 – Snowing hard	K.H.
"	25.12.17		Admitted 8 Evac 6 Duty 1 Remain 6 – Xmas Xmas festivities to patients & personnel – Brig. Gen. Ironside DSO visited at dinner time – to wish all ranks Compliments of Season.	K.H.
"	26.12.17		Admitted 1 Evac 1 Remain 6 – Preparations to move on 28th inst. Convalescent pts sent to GRENOGE Farm	K.H.
"	27.12.17		Evac. 11 Trans. to GRENOGE. 1 Duty, 1 Remain 0 – Closed Rest Station Transport by road to forward area – stopping overnight LEDERZELE area Lt. NAFEY MO R.E USA posted to temp duty with 163 Infantry Coy.	K.H.
ROUSBRUGGE	28.12.17		Admitted 1 off 5 O.R. Evac. 1 off. 5 O.R. Moved HQ by car to ROUSBRUGGE area. Personnel by train. Relieved W.17d 5.4 Tent. opens Divl Rest Stat at CROMBEKE X.22 a.46 from 2/3 Wessex Fld. Amb. 57 Div. Adv. party last night.	K.H.
CROMBEKE	29.12.17		Belgian huts – site being an old I.C.S. (French) – fitted with 200 B.C.S. beds & equipment. Taken over 102 Admitted 20 Evac. 10 Duty 12 Remain 100 – Slight thaw – Lt. Col. MA WINDER DSO. mentioned in Despatches	K.H.
"	30.12.17			K.H.
"	31.12.17		Admitted 8 Evac 7 Duty 2 Remain 99 No. 446712 Sgt. T. Woodcock " " "	K.H.

No 55 T.a.

COMMITTEE FOR THE
MEDICAL HISTORY OF THE WAR
Date —4 MAR. 1918

WAR DIARY or INTELLIGENCE SUMMARY

Army Form C. 2118

BELGIUM & FRANCE Sheet 19 1/40,000
55792 Vol 31
SHEET HAZEBROUCK 1/100,000

Place	Date	Hour	Summary of Events and Information	Remarks and references to Appendices
CROMBEKE	1.1.18		Admitted 7 Evac. 3 Transf. 1 Duty 20 Remain 82	Auth
"	2.1.18		Admitted 11 Evac. 6 " 2 Duty 9 Remain 78	Auth
"	3.1.18		" 13 " " " 5 " " 84	auth
"	4.1.18		" 17 " 4 " 13 " " 84	Maj. (T/Lt.Col.) M.G. WINDER DSO RAMC promoted Brevet Lt.Col. 4/1/18
"	5.1.18		" 26 " 10 " 4 " " 96	auth
"	6.1.18		" 19 " 11 " 16 " " 88	auth
"	7.1.18		" 29 " 11 " 3 " " 103	auth
"	8.1.18		" 21 " 9 " 6 " " 109	auth
"	9.1.18		" 36 " 8 " 9 " " 128	auth
"	10.1.18		" 19 " 9 " 7 " " 131	auth
"	11.1.18		" 38 " 11 " 10 " " 148	auth
"	12.1.18		" 27 " 17 " 21 " " 137	auth
"	13.1.18		" 40 " 16 " 8 " " 154	auth
"	14.1.18		" 14 " 8 " 9 " " 151	auth
"	15.1.18		" 25 " 7 " 4 " " 165	auth
"	16.1.18		" 18 " 4 " 12 " " 167	auth
"	17.1.18		" 29 " 8 " 2 " " 186	auth
"	18.1.18		" 21 " 13 " 4 " " 190	auth
"	19.1.18		" 39 " 9 " 3 " " 217	auth
"	20.1.18		" 27 " 19 " 14 " " 221 of which 113 are trench foot	auth
"	21.1.18		" 26 " 36 " 8 " " 203 " " 97 " " "	auth
"	22.1.18		" 18 " 13 " 6 " " 204	auth
"	23.1.18		" 27 " 7 " " " 218	auth
"	24.1.18		" 16 " 32 " 10 " " 192 " " 65 " " "	auth
"	25.1.18		" 15 " 25 " 12 " " 177	auth
"	26.1.18		" 12 " 27 " 19 " " 137 " " 28	auth

Army Form C. 2118

Vol 31
M/Winter
557A
Shut 19 Belgium & France 1/40,000

WAR DIARY
or
INTELLIGENCE SUMMARY

(Erase heading not required.)

Place	Date	Hour	Summary of Events and Information	Remarks and references to Appendices
CROMBEKE	27.1.18		Admitted 11 evacuated 22 died 4th remain 82. D in cent station & patients handed over to the 2 F.A. Moved to WAYENBURG camp Sheet 19 W.17 d.	
W.17.d.	28.1.18		Ambulance closed	
"	29.1.18		"	
"	30.1.18		"	
"	31.1.18		"	

COMMITTEE FOR THE
MEDICAL HISTORY OF THE WAR
Date -8 APR. 1918

WAR DIARY
or
INTELLIGENCE SUMMARY

Army Form C. 2118

5574A
Vol 32

(Erase heading not required.) BELGIUM & France Sheet 18 France ST QUENTIN

Place	Date	Hour	Summary of Events and Information	Remarks and references to Appendices
W17d	1.2.18		Ambulance closed	
"	2.2.18	nil	Capt F.E. TILLYARD RAMC TC joined station on strength	
"	3.2.18	nil	Rest station GRENOGE Farm closed, staff handed in tent subdivision rejoined Headquarters.	
"	4.2.18	nil		
"	5.2.18	nil		
"	6.2.18	nil		
"	7.2.18	nil		
"	8.2.18		Entrained at PROVEN 10.0 pm	
COUARCY	9.2.18		Detrained NOYON. Billeted at COUARCY 3 miles S.E. of NOYON. Ambulance closed	
"	10.2.18	nil		
"	11.2.18		Capt M. MULLIGAN RAMC TC joined & taken on strength	
"	12.2.18		Advance party took over chateau TIRLANCOURT 6 miles N of NOYON. Chateau to be made a Corps rest station	
"	13.2.18	nil		
TIRLANCOURT	14.2.18		Took over chateau for rest station officers 50 beds also 5 large french huts for a rest station for men to be increased to accommodate 500 as III rd Corps rest station, submitted necessary requisition to equip for this purpose.	
"	15.2.18		cleaning up	
"	16.2.18	nil		
"	17.2.18	nil		
"	18.2.18	nil	Capt DRYNAN RAMC TC posted for duty & taken on strength	
"	19.2.18	nil		
"	20.2.18	nil		

WAR DIARY
or
INTELLIGENCE SUMMARY

(Erase heading not required.)

Army Form C. 2118

57A M/Winter VV/32

Shelf is St QUENTIN 57/100

Place	Date	Hour	Summary of Events and Information	Remarks and references to Appendices
TIRANCOURT	21.2.18		nil	
"	22.2.18		2/Lt TILLYARD posted to 16th Entrenching Battn a struck off strength	
"	23.2.18		nil	
"	24.2.18		Capt DRYNAN posted to 56 TA & struck off strength	
"	25.2.18		Capt P.R. BELANGER posted from 12th Middlesex & taken on strength	
"	26.2.18		nil	
"	27.2.18		Ordered to lecture at 10.0 am at Fifth army School of Instruction on surgical arrangements of a F Amb	
"	28.2.18		nil	

55th Field Ambulance.

WAR DIARY
or
INTELLIGENCE SUMMARY

(Erase heading not required.)

Army Form C. 2118

4

SHEET 18 Frame ST QUENTIN

Place	Date	Hour	Summary of Events and Information	Remarks and references to Appendices
TIRANCOURT	1·3·18		nil	
"	2·3·18		Half heavy division 2 Horse drawn wagons 2 G.S. 4 lt motors detached for duty with 557A	
"	3·3·18		nil	
"	4·3·18		13 O.R. arrived as reinforcement	
"	5·3·18		nil	
"	6·3·18		Lecture at Fifth Army school of Instruction	
"	7·3·18		Capt W.H.L. McCARTHY R.A.M.C. S.R. posted to 547A as tn'd officer a'tng lt	
"	8·3·18		Capt MULLIGAN R.A.M.C. T.C. Reported open fm 40/fr 4/00 O.R.	
"	9·3·18		Blankets etc not yet issued sufficient for more over	
"	10·3·18		nil	
"	11·3·18		Equipment received is blankets & stretchers	
"	12·3·18		admitted 22 O.R.	
"	13·3·18		admitted 1·o/fr 11 O.R. remain 10/fr 33 O.R.	
"	14·3·18		admitted 2·o/fr 22 O.R. remain 3 " 55 "	
"	15·3·18		admitted 1·o/fr 17 O.R. remain 4 " 72 "	
"	16·3·18		admitted — 30 O.R. 3 " 94 " notified DDMS now recd/m 340 O.R.	
"	17·3·18		admitted — 21 O.R. 3 " 109 "	
"			Inspection of rest station by Corps Commander — D.D.M.S.	
"	18·3·18		admitted 3o/fr 26 O.R. remain 6 o/fr 128 O.R. DDMS. invited & instructed that Corps Commander reserves all main grounds of hosp to open sect of rest station, present hutting i.e, 5 huts is to be removed from present situation with the exception of one hut, to be converted for officers. Reported to R.E. officer with a view to action being taken in the matter.	

Army Form C. 2118
Vol 33

55 F.A.
M.Winter

SHEET 18 FRANCE 17 QUENTIN
" 17 " AMIENS

WAR DIARY or INTELLIGENCE SUMMARY
(Erase heading not required.)

Place	Date	Hour	Summary of Events and Information	Remarks and references to Appendices
TIRLANCOURT	19.3.18		Admitted 10 off 47 O.R. remained 6 off 164 O.R.	[initials]
"	20.3.18		Admitted 3 off 48 O.R. remained 9 off 185 O.R. at 2.30 pm received orders "Prepare for attack". This involved all cases not likely to be well in 4 days, being evacuated. 114 cases evacuated to C.C.S.	[initials]
"	21.3.18		Admitted 6 3 O.R. remained 10 off 118 O.R. at 6.0 am received the little notice. 7.0 am notified by D.D.M.S. that one of the C.C.S. receiving had closed & I should have to prepare to receive casualties. Arrangements made necessary for opening thirty & dealing with such cases.	[initials]
"	22.3.18		Admitted 20 off 40 O.R. remained 8 off 146 O.R. Enemy attack of 21st reached in front our defence line. Pt. COVERDALE A.S.C.M.T. motor cyclist evacuated wounded, one motor cycle & one Ford car smashed by shell. Influences demanded.	[initials]
"	23.3.18		Admitted 10 off 13 O.R. remained 8 off 120 O.R. Received warning to evacuate, even at 10.0 am. 4 off + to duty + to C.C.S. - O.R. 45 to duty 78 to C.C.S. reported closed by 3.0 pm. Ordered to move to LAGNY 4½ miles N.W. of NOYON & remain closed. Roads congested in parts, arrived 7.0 pm & reported to D.D.M.S. 9.30 p ordered to detail 2 off 25 O.R. of unit for duty at 46 C.C.S. NOYON these left 10.0 pm. CHATEAU TIRLANCOURT taken over by 14th Division as an A.D.S. stores left behind other than F.A. stores as no active transport available.	[initials]
LAGNY	24.3.18		remained waiting for orders.	
"	25.3.18		heard at 8.45 am a march to RESONS sur MATZ about 17 "	[initials]

Army Form C. 2118

Vol 33
55 ZA
(M.Winslow)

WAR DIARY
or
INTELLIGENCE SUMMARY
(Erase heading not required.)

Place	Date	Hour	Summary of Events and Information	Remarks and references to Appendices
			Sheet 21. BEAUVAIS 1/100,000	
	26.3.18		ordered to proceed to COMPIEGNE & orient with British wounded at French H.O.E. No 16 2 Klos S on Rue de Paris marched accordingly. Arrived 2.0 pm	Appx
COMPIEGNE	27.3.18		French evacuated all their cases & some British & left for CREIL. cleared about 30 city, a waiting room by train from COMPIEGNE. Owing to formation & enemy advance no hutter train expected. Arrangements made to meet them we 2y # MAC report here from Huty also 3 buses. All cases are sent on the French Hospital CREIL 28 kilometers distant. Place is used as a main dressing station & left as clear as possible. Capt McCARTHY M.C. evacuated with	Appx
"	28.3.18		All cases evacuated by car + bus to French Hosp at CREIL	Appx
"	29.3.18		trivial sick sent to duty, if fit other cases & wounded cases to French Hosp SENLIS wound to close a soon as got	Appx
"	30.3.18		cleared all cases & marched to CANLY to join 18th Div in transport. Reported to O/e Train. left 1 R.a.o 2 other ranks to remain 48 hours in case of French not resuming occupation, then to see that cases, & that might arrive, were directed on to SENLIS. 3 motor lorries were transferred 2A with trivial sick on tour.	Appx
—	31.3.18		Marched to LA NEUVILLE EN HEZ	Appx

160/2902

35th Field Ambulance.

WAR DIARY or INTELLIGENCE SUMMARY

Army Form C. 2118

557A
M Winder

Vol 34

Place	Date	Hour	Summary of Events and Information	Remarks and references to Appendices
	1.4.18		Marched from LANGUEVILLE en HEZ (BEAUVAIS sheet 21) to AUCHY LA MONTAGNE (sheet 17)	
	2.4.18		Marched to LEUILLY & bivouaced outside the village, reported to ADMS 18th Div	
AMIENS	3.4.18		Under orders of ADMS 18th Div marched to AMIENS and took over school on Southern bank at S. of ST ACHEUIL. Horse transport at E. of SALEUX ready to open as a dressing station for stretcher cases	
"	4.4.18		Four trained men remain from COMPIEGNE brought on the lorries	
"	5.4.18		Admitted 25 Officers 290 OR in attn. 21 sick, all evacuated, one tunisick remain. Capt RUNTING RAMC TC reported for duty temporary attachment 2nd Echelon arrived as reinforcement to [?] but thus [?] on [?] left dinner [?]	
"	6.4.18		Admitted 6 Officers 78 OR. evacuated 6 Off 60 OR 3 died 16 to duty and remain. Selected alternative site for dressing station at the school LONGPRE sent party to fit it	
"	7.4.18		Admitted 6 sick 4 to CCS 4 to duty. Capt RUNTING RAMC TC posted to 298 Field Amb Bde.	
"	8.4.18		Took over No 10 Temporary head Hosp at 10.0 am from 43 7A. Be started at ST. ACHEUIL. AMIENS. left holding party at school which remain closed. Few casualties being dealt with. Place in a CMDS.	
"	9.4.18		Admitted 2 offrs 16 sick 26 wounded (OR) 2 died 1 wounded 3 sick to duty, remainder [?] that [?] offrs 3 sick 14 wdd sick cases 3 d 13, 1 duty O.R 22 sick 143 wdd 22+136 to ccs, 1 duty 6 died	
"	10.4.18			

War Diary or Intelligence Summary

Army Form C. 2118

557.A.
M/Winder
Vol 34

Sheet 17 AMIENS 1/100,000

Place	Date	Hour	Summary of Events and Information	Remarks and references to Appendices
AMIENS	11.4.18		Admitted Off/r 2 sick 5 wounded O.R. 10 sick, 28 wounded, 3 O.R. died remainder to C.C.S	
"	12.4.18		Admitted Officer - wounded 3 - Died 1 C.C.S. 2 O.R. Admitted sick 7 wounded 53 - Died 3 C.C.S. 59. Lt. M.G. WINDER D.S.O. R.A.M.C. proceeded to H.Q. 18th Div. for temporary duty as A.D.M.S.	A.C. Hargill D.S.O. R.C.A.
"	13.4.18		Admitted Officers sick 1 wounded 10 Duty 1 C.C.S. 10. O.R. Admitted sick 8 wounded 98 Died 4 C.C.S. 102. Enemy dropped some 10 H.V. shells in immediate vicinity at 1.45 p.m. No damage to Dressing Station. Shelling recommenced 4 p.m. — one burst in garden at back of Dressing Station causing casualties: 72237 Pte. HUGHES H. severely wounded & evacuated, 46212 Sgt. HAGGER J.C. wounded	K.H.
"			31670 Sgt. BIRKINSHAW A.J. wounded 85007 - HOLLAND W.H. - J. remain at duty	
"	14.4.18		Admitted Officers sick 1 wounded 2 C.C.S. 3 D.R. Admitted sick 7 wounded 66 Died 2 C.C.S. 71 Intermittent H.V. Shelling throughout night close to Ecole de BAPAUME (Reserve Dress Station) - ordered by D.D.M.S to close same & open at LONGPRE. Complied by 5 P.M.	K.H.
"	15.4.18		Admitted Officers sick 2 wounded 5 C.C.S. 7 D.R. Admitted sick 8 wounded 63 Died 3 C.C.S. 68 Reserve in Reserve moved to LONGPRE	K.H.
"	16.4.18		Admitted Off/r 3 wounded O.R. 6 sick 36 wounded, 1 died all remainder evacuated Capt ROSS & M.C. proceeded — 15th to report for duty at base.	
"	17.4.18		Admitted O.R. 9 sick 47 wounded 3 died remainder evacuated	
"	18.4.18		Admitted Off/r 1 sick 52 wounded O.R. 16 sick - 687 wounded evacuated all less this draft all cases of wounded were Gas shell bothered with exception of 37. had difficulty in evacuation cars not sufficient 20 cars attached from D.M.S. 4th Army to assist.	
"	19.4.18		Admitted Off/r 1 sick 28 wounded O.R. 15 sick 319 wounded 6 died remainder evacuated 312 of these were gassed. Handed over Dressing Station to 25.7.A. 8th Division marched to LONGPRE 2 miles NN AHRENS. Remain closed School taken over ready to open forthwith	

1875 Wt. W593/826 1,000,000 4/15 J.B.C. & A. A.D.S.S./Forms/C. 2118.

Army Form C. 2118

5574
MMinden Vol 34

WAR DIARY
or
INTELLIGENCE SUMMARY
(Erase heading not required.)

Instructions regarding War Diaries and Intelligence Summaries are contained in F. S. Regs., Part II. and the Staff Manual respectively. Title Pages will be prepared in manuscript.

Place	Date	Hour	Summary of Events and Information	Remarks and references to Appendices
LONGPRÉ	20.4.18		One tent subdivision sent to ENDS. Sheet AMIENS h 1/40,000	
"	21.4.18		LT SIMONDS M.O.R.C posted to 1st DAC. Horse transport required replaced Sheet 62.D.	
"	22.4.18		Ambulance closed	
"	23.4.18		closed	
"	24.4.18		closed	
"	25.4.18		closed	
"	26.4.18		closed	
"	27.4.18		closed	
"	28.4.18		marched to MONTIGNY with 55 Brigade group. Reported to ADMS 2 Australian Div to which brigade is attached	
MONTIGNY	29.4.18		Visited No 5 Aust F.A. at GRANVILLERS to arrange to take over.	
"	30.4.18		Took over forward area. in R.A.P., D24a.2.8, D12d.2.8, D21c.5.2. + R.A.P. area church in BRESLE. Also relay post D17c.4.5 + motor loading post D16c.2.3	

Army Form O. 1784

Claim for Indemnification—Officers.

RETURN of Baggage, Camp Equipage, or Horse Equipment lost on Service by* Lieut & Qr Mr H. F. Jordan on† 27th February 1918 at‡ Firses Camp under the following circumstances§ Kit kept in Hut occupied by about 40 Officers. Warning of fire given when Hut was blazing furiously fanned by brisk breeze which prevented any attempt at salvage.

Articles separately detailed for the loss of which compensation is claimed (to be distinguished under the same classes as those by which they are described in Schedules A and B).		Actual cost of each article ǁ			Actual value at the time of loss see Allowance Regulations.			Remarks
		£	s.	d.	£	s.	d.	
Tunic Whipcord	1	5	15	0	5	15	0	
Breeches pair	2	3	13	6	3	10	0	
Belt Sam Brown	1		12	6		10	0	
Boots ankle prs	1	1	15	0	1	10	0	R49
Boots Gum	1		13	9		13	9	
Spurs	1		5	3		5	3	
Waistcoat warm	1	1	5	0	1	0	0	
Waterproof Sheet	1		4	6		5	0	
Coat British warm	1	6	0	0	5	10	0	
Razor	1	1	1	0	1	0	0	
Towels	2		3	6		3	0	
Hair Brush	1		6	0		5	0	
Comb	1		1	6		1	0	
Tooth Brush	1		1	4		1	3	
Shaving —	1		4	6		3	0	
Holdall	1		5	0		5	0	
Shirts	2		18	0		15	0	
Collars	2		3	0		2	6	
Ties	2		4	0		4	0	
Drawers	2		15	0		12	6	
Total amount ... £		22	11	0				Carried Forward

Recommended that this claim be paid
R Hampton Major General

The foregoing is a true and correct statement of my loss on the occasion referred to; and I hereby certify, upon my honour, that the actual cost of each article, and its true value at the time of loss are correctly stated according to the best of my judgment and belief; that I was not at the time deviating in any respect from the Orders of the General or other Officer Commanding; that I have neither received nor applied for indemnification on account of the above loss through any other channel than that in which the present claim is submitted, that indemnification is not obtainable from any other source, and that I have re-equipped myself for service with the articles in respect of which this claim is made.

(To be signed by the Officer making the claim) H. F. Jordan Lt & Qr Mr
10th Bn Essex Regiment

I hereby certify, that I have particularly examined and enquired into the facts and circumstances of the before-mentioned loss, and that I have every reason to believe the same to be correctly and justly stated.

(To be signed by the Officer under whose immediate command the claimant is serving.) A. S. Green Major
Commanding 10th (Service) Battn The Essex Regt

* Appointment, rank, and name to be inserted. † Date to be inserted. ‡ Place to be inserted. § Here detail minutely the particulars attending the loss. ǁ The transmission of the tradesmen's bills in support of the actual cost will facilitate the adjustment of the claim.

Army Form O. 1784

Claim for Indemnification—Officers.

RETURN of Baggage, Camp Equipage, or Horse Equipment lost on Service by* _Lieut & Q'r M' H. S. Jordan_ on† _29th February 1916_ at‡ _Heron Camp_ under the following circumstances §

Articles separately detailed for the loss of which compensation is claimed (to be distinguished under the same classes as those by which they are described in Schedules A and B).	Actual cost of each article ‖			Actual value at the time of loss see Allowance Regulations.			Remarks
	£	s.	d.	£	s.	d.	
Brought Forward				22	17	0	
Socks pair	2		6		2	0	
Handkerchiefs	3	4	6		4	0	
Shirts pair	1	7	6		5	0	
Electric Torch	1	15	6		13	0	
Binoculars	1	2 10	0	2	5	0	Ordnance ! H.J.St
Puttees pair	1	9	6		4	6	
Pistol case	1	10	6		8	6	
Ammunition Pouch	1	5	0		4	0	
Waterbottle & Sling	1	1 10	0	1	5	0	
Haversack	1	19	6		15	0	
Braces pair	1	6	6		6	6	
Mess Tin	1	12	6		10	6	
Shoes canvas	1	10	6		8	0	
Valise Straps pair	1	6	0		4	0	
Bath rubber	1	5	0	1	0	0	
Recommended that this claim be paid							
Total amount ... £		29	4	0			£29-4-0 H.J.St

Major General Commanding 18th Division

The foregoing is a true and correct statement of my loss on the occasion referred to; and I hereby certify, upon my honour, that the actual cost of each article, and its true value at the time of loss are correctly stated according to the best of my judgment and belief; that I was not at the time deviating in any respect from the Orders of the General or other Officer Commanding; that I have neither received nor applied for indemnification on account of the above loss through any other channel than that in which the present claim is submitted, that indemnification is not obtainable from any other source, and that I have re-equipped myself for service with the articles in respect of which this claim is made.

(To be signed by the Officer making the claim) _H. S. Jordan Lieut & Q'r M'_

I hereby certify, that I have particularly examined and enquired into the facts and circumstances of the before-mentioned loss, and that I have every reason to believe the same to be correctly and justly stated.

(To be signed by the Officer under whose immediate command the claimant is serving.) _A. S. Green Major_
Commanding 10th (Service) Battⁿ The Essex Regt

---

* Appointment, rank, and name to be inserted.   † Date to be inserted.   ‡ Place to be inserted.   § Here detail minutely the particulars attending the loss.   ‖ The transmission of the tradesmen's bills in support of the actual cost will facilitate the adjustment of the claim.

18th Div. No. Q.319

Subject:- Indemnification Claims, Officers.

53rd Inf. Bde.

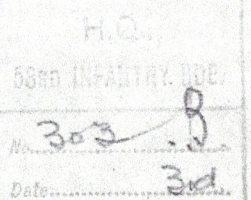

Reference attached claim. - No depreciation for the following articles has been deducted:-

    Tunic, whipcord.
    Boots, gum.
    Gloves.

If these were new, a certificate to that effect must be made; if not, depreciation in value must be allowed.

This officer has claimed up to full amount of kit allowed. Presumably, he was wearing one set at the time of fire.. In which case, only one of each article should be claimed for.

2/5/18.

                              Major,
D.A.Q.M.G., 18th Division.

P.T.O

2

10 Essex/
    forwarded

3/5/18

71606

[signature]
Staff Capt

O. C.
10th (S) Bn. The Essex Regt.

Reference attached Claim.

I certify that Tunic lost in Fire was only purchased in December 1917, and had not been worn in France as it was made for Flying Corps and had to be altered and fitted with new buttons consequently costing more than value claimed and was equal to new.

The boots, gum, and gloves were new, only being received from ordnance 2 or 3 days before the fire, and ordnance prices have been claimed.

Two pair of boots were lost but, as only 1 pair can be claimed for, this, has now been corrected.

H. Jordan
Lieut.
10th Bn Essex Regt

4/5/18.

14 9/2983.

No. 55 ∗ G.

55 Field Amb.

Army Form C. 2118

557A
Winder Vol 35

WAR DIARY or INTELLIGENCE SUMMARY
(Erase heading not required.)

Sheet AMIENS 17 1/100,000
Sheet 62 d 1/20,000

Place	Date	Hour	Summary of Events and Information	Remarks and references to Appendices
FRANVILLERS	1.5.18		Turned hut complete 30% aptd Monhead gunshot to FRANVILLERS, took over ADS there	appx
"	2.5.18		All receiving done at MDS MONTIGNY. Large number of such reporting. FRANVILLERS being only one wounded in last 24 hours. Selected site C.22.a.7.2 as an alternative site in case of village being heavily shelled & becoming untenable. Reason to be fitted with a newly beating sections at present all quiet	appx
"	3.5.18			appx
"	4.5.18	4.0pm	40°F S/tr morning. Temperature asked ADMS loan of one officer to carry one man sent from 54 FA. sent there across to alternative site See 3rd	appx
"	5.5.18		Visited RAPs. Horrible evacuation must be along AIBERT. AMIENS road if the road is damaged too heavily cases will have to be carried probably via D.17.d. 17.c. 16.d to carr.	appx
"	6.5.18		18th Division coming up	appx
"	7.5.18		Capt R I CLAUSEN joined a detach. in strength, took over RAP (2 det) at 17.d 2.9. for evacuation cases of 54 Bde. Command of rector handed to 18th Division	appx
"	8.5.18		LT HICKEY W. RAMC. T.F. joined & taken on strength	appx
"	9.5.18		Some shelling in village, shell burst in billet Pte MILLS H & NASH killed Capt THOMAS Pte PILKINGTON, BOTTELL wounded & evacuated. Pte FAIRLESS & Pte AMPION wounded at duty 11.0 pm 8th	appx
"	10.5.18		All personnel moved up at C.22.a.7.2. necessary drawing station parties day & night making ADS at about FRANVILLERS	appx

Army Form C. 2118

Vol 35

WAR DIARY
or
INTELLIGENCE SUMMARY
(Erase heading not required.)

557A
(Winter)

Instructions regarding War Diaries and Intelligence Summaries are contained in F.S. Regs., Part II. and the Staff Manual respectively. Title Pages will be prepared in manuscript.

Place	Date	Hour	Summary of Events and Information	Remarks and references to Appendices
FRANVILLERS	11.5.18		hot noon even though	
"	12.5.18		nil	Appx
"	13.5.18		Visited R.A.P. 53rd brigade	Appx
"	14.5.18		Capt R.J. CLAUSEN posted to reserve army Musketry school & struck off strength	Appx
"	15.5.18		10 reinforcement O.R. joined	Appx
"	16.5.18		nil	Appx
"	17.5.18		Pte MINTER killed shell fire in BRESLE	Appx
"	18.5.18		nil	Appx
"	19.5.18		Division on right attacked & took VILLE-sur-ANCRE, 18th Division raiding at same time about	Appx
"	20.5.18		70 casualties passed through	Appx
"	21.5.18		D.D.M.S. visited A.D.S. and collecting post	Appx
"	22.5.18		nil	Appx
"	23.5.18		nil	Appx
"	24.5.18		forward post taken over by 5th Lond 7A (47Div) 7.0am A.D.S. FRANVILLERS 10.0am	Appx
			Handed over to O.C. 5th Lond 7A. 7A moved back complete to WOOD B.15.l.	
			closed.	
B.15 l.	25.5.18		Ambulance closed	Appx
"	26.5.18		closed	Appx
"	27.5.18		30 reinforcements joined	Appx
"	28.5.18		nil	Appx
"	29.5.18		nil	Appx
"	30.5.18		Visited M.D.S. VADENCOURT & arranged to take over from 58 Div on 1st June	Appx
"	31.5.18			Appx

18th Division

Forwarded

M Sackville
Comdg 53rd Inf Bde. Brig Genl

7.5.18

[Stamp: HEADQUARTERS 18TH DIVISION No. Q4943 10 MAY 1918]

"A" Form
MESSAGES AND SIGNALS.

Army Form C. 2121
(in pads of 100).

TO	3 Corps R.T.C.
	~~SS Bn~~

Sender's Number.	Day of Month.	In reply to Number.	AAA
G8/7	11		

Send up Capt NICHOLAS The Buffs to-day if possible aaa He is urgently required by his Battalion aaa from 3 Corps RTC rpt SS Rein C/o ...

From 18 Div
Place
Time 12/2/1

Headquarters,

18th Division.

X/3046

Reference your No. Q.898, dated 27/4/18, will you please state the reason Lt. T.V.S. Twentyman, M.C., ceased to be employed as 2nd-in-Command of C/82 Battery.

General Headquarters,
9. May, 1918.

Lieut.

for Military Secretary
to Commander-in-Chief.

160/3076.

COMMITTEE FOR THE
MEDICAL HIST...
Date 7 AUG 1918

35" + a.

June 1918

WAR DIARY / INTELLIGENCE SUMMARY

Army Form C. 2118

Sheet 11 LENS 1/100,000
Trench 57 D 1/40,000

557 A.D. V.A. 36

Place	Date	Hour	Summary of Events and Information	Remarks and references to Appendices
VADENCOURT	1.6.18		Took over M.D.S. from 58th Div. at 10.0 am. Horse transport, less necessary wagon, left at Bishs.	
"	2.6.18		Admitted 19, 4 evacuated wd. O.R. admitted 58 S&W. evacuated 52	
"	3.6.18		Admitted 2 off, evacuated 2. O.R. admitted 73 S&W evacuated 68	
"	4.6.18		LT HENLEY posted to 8th 2 surveys attached off Army Ch	
"	5.6.18		One officer wd. & evacuated O.R. 34 admitted S&W 4 34 evacuated	
"	6.6.18		O.R. admitted S&W 23 evac 24. Capt SENIOR evacuated sick	
"	7.6.18		Admitted 4 evacuated 2 officers. O.R. admitted 47 evac 33 now receiving Sicks in	
"	8.6.18		Admitted R&W 29 evacuated 24 14 sick in	
"	9.6.18		Admitted & evac 2 officers O.R. S&W 31 admitted 28 evac 16 sick remain	
"	10.6.18		Admitted & evac 1 sick officer. O.R. admitted S&W 36 evac 34 15 sick remain	
"	11.6.18		Officer 4 admitted & evacuated O.R. 57 S&W admitted 52 evac 14 sick remain	
"	12.6.18		Admitted S&W 30 evacuated 29. 14 sick remain	
"	13.6.18		Admitted 28 evacuated 27. 8 sick remain	
"	14.6.18		Two officer admitted sick & evacuated. 24 O.R. 24 evacuated 2 sick remain	
"	15.6.18		3 officer admitted S&W & evacuated O.R. 34 admitted 33 evacuated 2 sick remain	
"	16.6.18		2 officer admitted & evacuated O.R. 39 admitted 37 evacuated 3 sick remain	
"	17.6.18		Admitted 2 evacuated 1 officer O.R. admitted 17 evacuated 16 3 sick remain	
"	18.6.18		Admitted 1 office evacuated 1 O.R. admitted 34 evacuated 34 4 sick remain	
"	19.6.18		Admitted 2 off, evacuated 2 O.R. admitted 30 evacuated 30 3 sick remain	
"	20.6.18		Admitted & evacuated 3 officers D.R. admitted 29 evacuated 26 5 sick remain	
"	21.6.18		Admitted & evacuated 4 off O.R. admitted 28 evacuated 26 7 sick remain	

27

Army Form C. 2118

WAR DIARY
or
INTELLIGENCE SUMMARY
(Erase heading not required.)

557.A. Vol 36
mWwinder

SKETCH LENS 1/40,000
France 57D 1/40,000

Place	Date	Hour	Summary of Events and Information	Remarks and references to Appendices
VADENCOURT	22.6.18		admitted 41 O.R. 9 evacuated 6 seabies remain	Appx
"	23.6.18		Capt H.S. EVANS R.A.M.C.S.R. joined from 34.H. strength on strength 21/6/18 admitted 8 evacuated 5 officer admitted O.R. 45 evacuated 42 8 seabies remain	Appx Appx
"	24.6.18		Capt H.S. BERRY R.A.M.C. reported for duty 22nd & taken on strength admitted O.R. 6 evacuated 6. O.R. admitted 30 evacuated 48 10 seabies remain	Appx Appx
"	25.6.18		admitted 4 evacuated 5 officer. O.R. admitted 47 evacuated 46 10 seabies remain	Appx Appx
"	26.6.18		admitted 4 evacuated 2 officer O.R. admitted 56 evacuated 55 8 seabies remain Capt LOVELL R.A.M.C. posted to 12 C.C.S. & struck off strength 25th	Appx Appx
"	27.6.18		admitted 9 evacuated 3 off 68 O.R. 7 seabies remain	Appx
"	28.6.18		admitted 4 evacuated 2 off 65 O.R. 5 seabies remain	Appx
"	29.6.18		admitted 9 evacuated 9 officer O.R. admitted 72 evacuated 67 7 seabies remain	Appx
"	30.6.18		admitted 9 evacuated 3 officer O.R. admitted 87 evacuated 84 5 seabies remain	Appx

140/3131.

No. 55 T.a.

July 1918

COMMITTEE FOR THE
MEDICAL HISTORY
Date -6 SEP

WAR DIARY or INTELLIGENCE SUMMARY

Army Form C. 2118

Vol 37

Place	Date	Hour	Summary of Events and Information	Remarks and references to Appendices
VADENCOURT	1.7.18		Anurer attach by left brigade in conjunction with division on left starting 9.30 pm	
			admitted offrs W.5 S.dl 3 all evacuated O.R. W.121 S.82 evacuated 110 W.D 82 sick 5 sick remain	
"	2.7.18		Offrs sick O.R. admitted W.67 S.16 evacuated W.60 S.75. 4 sick remain	
			Capt H.S. BERRY posted to 7th Brigade & truck off strength 2/7/18.	
"	3.7.18		admitted S.W.3 S. officer evacuated name O.R. admitted 78 W. 75 S.S. evacuated 64.W.72.S. 7 sick remain	
"	4.7.18		admitted & evacuated one officer. admitted O.R. 50 S. 30 W. evacuated 46 S. 31 W. 11 sick remain	
"	5.7.18		admitted & evacuated one officer. admitted O.R. 39 evacuated 37 10 sick remain	
"	6.7.18		admitted & evacuated 7 officer. admitted O.R. 39 evacuated 38 11 sick remain	
"	7.7.18		admitted & evacuated 1 officer. admitted O.R. 34 evacuated 33 8 sick remain	
"	8.7.18		admitted O.R. 38 evacuated 36 8 sick remain	
"	9.7.18		admitted & evacuated 1 offr. O.R. admitted 58 evacuated 54 7 sick remain	
"	10.7.18		LT CAREY. W.II MORE. Lts. joined on strength	
			admitted O.R. 23 evacuated 23 7 sick remain	
"	11.7.18		admitted & evacuated 1 officer, admitted O.R. 38 evacuated 37 3 sick remain	
"	12.7.18		admitted 28 O.R. evacuated 27 nil remain	
			arrived on 11th details and main body above & completed taking over by 6.0 pm	
			7A endorsed. Horse transport by road & arrived at DREUIL LES MOLLIENS transport by 47 Division	
DREUIL LES MOLLIENS	13.7.18.		opened hospital in huts for 1st Brigade sick	
"	14.7.18		admitted & evacuated 4 O.R	
"	15.7.18		admitted & evacuated officer admitted O.R. 12 evacuated 3 remain 9	
"	16.7.18		admitted 5 evacuated 4 remain 10. Major RICHARDS 14 days leave	
"	17.7.18		admitted 18 evacuated 2 remain 25	

WAR DIARY or INTELLIGENCE SUMMARY

Army Form C. 2118

5577A
Vol 37
M Munro

(Erase heading not required.)

Shot AMIENS.

Place	Date	Hour	Summary of Events and Information	Remarks and references to Appendices
DREUIL LES MOLLIENS	18.7.18		admitted 7 evacuated 3 remaining 24	appx
"	19.7.18		admitted 6 evacuated 2 remaining 19	appx
"	20.7.18		admitted 9 evacuated 1 officer admitted OR 3 evacuated 2 remaining 13	appx
"	21.7.18		LT CAREY M.O.R.C. USA posted to 82 Bd R74 19a & struck off strength	appx
"			admitted 8 evacuated 3 remain 12	appx
"	22.7.18		admitted 10 evacuated 8 remain 11	appx
"	23.7.18		admitted 10 evacuated 3 remain 16	appx
"	24.7.16		admitted 4 evacuated 0 remain 17	appx
"	25.7.18		admitted 4 evacuated 7 remain 12	appx
"	26.7.18		admitted 9 wounded 2 remain 7 Shots fired outside of 3.7A m/c	appx
"	27.7.18		admitted 2 remain 9	appx
"	28.7.18		admitted 9 evacuated 1 officer admitted OR 2 evacuated 3 remain 4 Major E.B. BOOTH 258 Rame Ry joined 27.7.18 & taken on strength	appx
"	29.7.18		admitted 7 evacuated 8 remain 3	appx
"	31.7.18		admitted 20 evacuated 23 hospital closed unit entrained them transported by rail & moved to FRECHENCOURT	appx
FRECHENCOURT	31.7.18		remain closed no accommodation available to open in	appx

164/3259.

No. 53 & a.b.

Aug. 1918

COMMITTEE FOR THE
MEDICAL HISTORY OF THE WAR
Date 9 NOV 1910

Army Form C. 2118

55 Field Ambulance
Vol 38

WAR DIARY
or
INTELLIGENCE SUMMARY

(Erase heading not required.)

Sheet AMIENS
FRANCE

Place	Date	Hour	Summary of Events and Information	Remarks and references to Appendices
FRECHENCOURT	1.8.18		Remain closed	
"	2.8.18		Closed	
MONTIGNY	3.8.18		Moved from FRECHENCOURT & took over from B.17 & 4.9. Cmfn Walking wounded station	
"	4.8.18		Lt. Col. McKINDER D.S.O. Regrs. proceeded to Div. H.Q. on Temporary duty as A.D.M.S. Cars shifted to form D.R.S. Accommodation 100 patients — D.D.M.S. visited	
"	5.8.18		Instructions to draw up stores to holding hundreds a grand Canon in case of emergency — to deal with 1000 men	
"	6.8.18		Admitted 12 Remain 12 — D.R.S. 4 A.P. tents issued by T.S Corps — not to be pitched. Bearers to proceed over A.P. tents pitched at night	
"	7.8.18		" 15 C & S 1 Remain 26 — handed to be ready for wounded tomorrow — A.P. tents pitched at night	
"	8.8.18		" 146 C & S 115 Duty 19 Remain 38 — Battle opened — walking wounded began to arrive 7.30 am	
"			" continued all day — highest persons after midday for 3 or 4 hours — there passed cases than been expected — 500 in all, of which about 230 from 12 Div. High percentage than Corps slightly high 7/165 3 off. 16 O.R. from 58 Div. 5 O.R. from 12 Div. 2 Off. 14 O.R. from 33 Amer. Div. 28 lorries — arrived to assist in clearing wounded.	
"	9.8.18		Admitted 1618 CCS 1412 Duty 88 Remain 156 — Accommodation taxed for large number my dept wounded detained for 24 m and returned to duty	
"	10.8.18			
"	11.8.18		Admitted 1110 CCS 949 Duty 81 Remain 136	
"	12.8.18		" 375 CCS 328 Duty 114 Remain 69 Bearer division regrouped	
"	13.8.18		" 125 CCS 89 Duty 44 Remain 59	
"			" 70 CCS 65 Duty 22 Remain 42. 1 off in 33 American div returned to own unit 10 hours ordered to report back to H.M.T.O.	
"	14.8.18		Admitted 81 CCS 75 Duty 9 Remain 27. Working party 50 men cleaning same st at BONNAY to make a new Enfm Walking Wounded station	
"	15.8.18		Admitted 163 CCS 149 Duty 9 Remain 32	
"	16.8.18		" 60 CCS 40 Duty 5 CRS 5 Remain 42	
"	17.8.18		" 39 CCS 31 Duty 8 CRS 22 Remain 20	

WAR DIARY or INTELLIGENCE SUMMARY

Army Form C. 2118

557A Vol 38
MJ Winder

Sheet AMIENS 1/100,000
62D 1/100 ALBERT combined with 1/40

Place	Date	Hour	Summary of Events and Information	Remarks and references to Appendices
MONTIGNY	18.8.18		admitted 36 CCS 27 duty 3 CRS 3 remain 23	Appx
	19.8.18		admitted 19 CCS 11 duty 3 CRS 5 remain 23 Leave for W.W. Leave 2, rejoined their Appx	Appx
	20.8.18		admitted 19 CCS 23 duty 6 CRS 4 remain 9 closed at MONTIGNY removed all equipmt	Appx
			& rested in a large barn at N end of BONNAY for walking wounded + gun centre slight cases	
BONNAY	21.8.18		admitted 4 CCS 4 CRS 9, remain closed	Appx
	22.8.18		III corp attached 4.40am	Appx
	23.9.18		admitted 1642 evacuated 1503 to DRS° 68 duty 53 remained 22	Appx
	24.8.18		admitted 836 evacuated 746 DRS 33 duty 58 remained 39	Appx
	25.8.18		admitted 647 evacuated 536 DRS 43 duty 64 remained 36	Appx
	26.8.18		admitted 681 evacuated 582 DRS 40 duty 92 remained 3	Appx
			CWW station to be established under canvas in front of MEAULTE E.18 b 2.8 shut 62D	
	27.8.18		admitted 502 evacuated 442 duty 63 remain nil closed & reopened at E.18 b 2.8	Appx
			at 12 noon.	
E.18 b 2.8	28.8.18		admitted 521 evacuated 471 duty 50 remain nil	Appx
	29.8.18		admitted 455 evacuated 402 duty 62 remain nil	Appx
	30.8.18		admitted 162 evacuated 169 duty 13 remain nil Advance post 7.0 am to	Appx
			pitch new CWW station at MARICOURT A.21 a 8.9 ALBERT combined sheet opened new	
			CWW.3 at 4.0 pm	
A.21a 8.9	31.8.18		admitted 299 evacuated 284 duty 15 remain nil	Appx

140/34.01.

55th F.A.

Part 108

WAR DIARY or INTELLIGENCE SUMMARY

Army Form C. 2118

Vol 39

Sheet 62c 1/40,000 55 7A 1/40,000 ALBERT

Place	Date	Hour	Summary of Events and Information	Remarks and references to Appendices
A.21.a.8.9	1.9.18		admitted 441 evacuated 416 duty 24 remain nil	Antre
"	2.9.18		admitted 706 evacuated 649 D.R.S. 25 duty 32 remain nil .S/Sgt PATERSON & Pte WOLSTENCROFT awarded MM	Antre
"	3.9.18		admitted 795 evacuated 765 D.R.S. 8 duty 22 " " MM presented August	Antre
"	4.9.18		admitted 179 evacuated 169 D.R.S. 2 duty 8 " "	Antre
"	5.9.18		admitted 98 evacuated 93 D.R.S. 1 duty 4 " " 18th division in	Antre
"	6.9.18		1st beaver division 55 rejoined Hy.	Antre
"	7.9.18		admitted 510 evacuated 477 D.R.S. 8. duty 25	Antre
"			admitted 274 evacuated 253 D.R.S. 19 duty 2 advance heart to forward	
			at 6.30 am to pitch CWS station at D 20 c central sheet 62 c near NURLU-PEROANNE road	Antre
D20c central	8.9.18		admitted 303 evacuated 290. 13duty. remain nil	Antre
62 c sheet	9.9.18		admitted 202 evacuated 193 duty 8 remain 1	Antre
"	10.9.18		admitted 88 evacuated 81 duty 8 remain nil	Antre
"	11.9.18		admitted 158 evacuated 150 duty 8 remain nil	Antre
"	12.9.18		admitted 45 evacuated 45 Lines mens 1 to each division 11 to P.O.W cation	Antre
"	13.9.18		admitted 33 evacuated 29 duty 4	Antre
"	14.9.18		admitted 43 evacuated 41 duty 2	Antre
"	15.9.18		admitted 49 evacuated 48 duty 1	Antre
"	16.9.18		admitted 43 evacuated 40 duty 3	Antre
"	17.9.18		admitted 77 evacuated 74 duty 3 beaver division moved up to work	Antre
			under OC 547A	
"	18.9.18		4 officers 200 R. attached III corps attached 5.20 am with 4 divisions admitted 413 evacuated 408 duty 5	Antre

WAR DIARY
or
INTELLIGENCE SUMMARY

(Erase heading not required.)

Army Form C. 2118

Sheet 62 c / 40,000 Sheet 57 c
5679 / Vol 39
M.W.Walder

Place	Date	Hour	Summary of Events and Information	Remarks and references to Appendices
D20c until	19/9/18		Admitted 1631 evacuated 1566 duty 65. Pte ROSE & GREENWOOD wounded & died on way down. Pte CARNEGIE & ANDISON wounded & evacuated	ATP note
"	20/9/18		admitted 498 evacuated 471 duty 26 died 1. Pte KNOWLES & COOPER wounded evacuated	ATP
"	21/9/18		admitted 160 evacuated 147 duty 13	ATP
"	22/9/19		admitted 846 evacuated 882 duty 36. Handed over CWWs to 38 FA at 2.10 pm and moved to MOISLAINS C17d 7,9.	ATP
C17d 7.9.	23.9.18		open up to 30 cases sick of 18th D invision	ATP
"	24.9.18		admitted no sick	ATP
"	25-9-18		admitted 14 sick 1 wounded. Evacuated 3 sick 1 wounded. Kept sick. Moved to COMBLES T.28 & 33	Results
COMBLES	26-9-18		Moved D.R.S. Admitted Nil. Beacon Annexe opened.	
"	27-9-18		A.D.M.S. Order No 105 received ordering No 55 F.A. to take charge of forward evacuation during forthcoming operations. Reconnaissance of forward area carried out.	
ST.EMILIE	28-9-18		Moved Mobile Ambulance to ST EMILIE E24, B.2.7. Area kept knowful where remained at COMBLES. Capts S. EVANS. R.A.M.C. proceed to 7th QUEENS for temporary duty. Lieut B. KING to 7th EAST KENTS for temporary duty.	order not attached
"	29-9-18		6.50 A.M Offensive Commenced. Heavy division 2 Officers 14 signallers the line. A.D.S. established at ST EMILIE P24. T.2.7. Ford Car Post at RONSSOY. F.15 c 9.3 evacuating to LARGE CAR POST at EPEHY F.1.c 9,7. from thence to A.D.Spm the castle & M.D.S. VILLERS FAUCON. Walking wounded by lorry from A.D.S. to Corps W. Post at D.D.C.	
			Casualties: Capt. H.S. EVANS, R.A.M.C. — Wounded at duty	
			R.A.M.C. 55th P.A. I.O.R. — Wounded evacuated	
	30-9-18		Casualties heavy. Tungk A.P.S Officers 4 O.R. 177. Ford Car Post established at TOMBOIS FARM F.n. B 2 6 - LARGE CAR POST at RONSSOY F.15 c 9.3 evacuated to M.D.S. at VILLERS FAUCON 55th P.A Killed No 69703 Pte KAY J. Wounded O.R. 5 (3 evacuated) Casualties RAMC 55th PA	CULL
			Casualties heard Tungk A.D.S Officers 2 — O.R. 113.	CULL

SECRET.   Copy No 10

55 FIELD AMBULANCE ORDERS No. 1.

MAP REFERENCE Sheet 62C, 1/40000

1. O.C's 54th, 55th & 56th Bearer Divisions will be responsible for the evacuation of wounded of 54th, 55th & 53rd Brigades respectively. Six stretchers, one red cross flag & one water tin per squad will be taken. Two squads with one pair stretcher wheels will be posted to each Battalion by Y-Z night.

2. As the attack progresses an A.D.S. will be formed. Prior to this cases will be cleared to Ford Car Post, where a M.O. of 55 Fd Amb will be in charge. When A.D.S. opens a M.O. of Bearer Division Surgeons will establish his H.Q. &, & will be responsible for work of Ford Car Post.

3. Close liaison will be kept by O.C. Bearers with their respective Brigades. Report centre of O.C. 55 Fd Amb will be at ST EMILIE, E14b 2.7.

4. Rendezvous for all Cars ST EMILIE, E14b 2.7. Ford Cars to report at Zero hour. Large cars at Zero + 2 hours.

5. Horse Ambulances less those of 55 Fd Amb, will rendezvous at TINCOURT WOOD by 6 a.m. Y-Z night.

28.9.18
9 A.M.
                                                            Elliott
                                                        Major R.A.M.C.,
Copies to :-   O.C, 55 FIELD AMBULANCE

1-2   O.C's 54 & 56 Fld. Ambulances
3-5   B.C's Bearer Divisions 54, 55 & 56 Fld Ambulances
6   A.D.M.S
7-9   H.Q. 53, 54 & 55 Infantry Brigades
10-11   War Diary
12.   Office Copy

1407/3481

No. 567.a

Oct 1915

COMMITTEE FOR THE
MEDICAL HISTORY OF THE WAR
6 MAR. 1919
Date

4 55 3rd Auth
Army Form C. 2118
55. F.A VOL. 40
Sheet 62. e.
1/20,000
57D 40600

WAR DIARY
or
INTELLIGENCE SUMMARY
(Erase heading not required.)

Place	Date	Hour	Summary of Events and Information	Remarks and references to Appendices
ST EMILIE	1/10/18		Under orders from A.D.M.S. handed over forward area to 2/2 Northumberland Field Ambulance. Relief completed at 23.45 o'c. All transport at COMBLES. Orders for personnel to embus at 9 a.m. tomorrow	
VADENCOURT	2/10/18		Ambulance moved to VADENCOURT CHATEAU. Move completed at 16.00 o'c.	
"	3/10/18		Accommodation for 40 cases provided. Admissions nil	
"	4/10/18		Capt. R.B. Stewart proceeded on leave to U.K. Admissions 12. C.C.S. 8. Remaining 4	
"	5/10/18		Admitted 38. C.C.S. 19. Remaining 23	
"	6/10/18		Admitted 11. C.C.S. 10. Remaining 24	
"	7/10/18		Admitted Officers 2. O.R. 4. C.C.S. Officers 2. O.R. 8. Remaining 20	
"	8/10/18		Admitted 6. To duty 3. Remaining 23	
"	9/10/18		Admitted 4. C.C.S. 4. Remaining 23	
"	10/10/18		Admitted 11. To duty 4. C.C.S. 4. Remaining 26	
"	11/10/18		Admitted 7. To duty 7. C.C.S. 1. Remaining 25	
"	12/10/18		Handed over ambulance to Major Booth D.S.O. 4 under orders of D.M.S. 4th Army. Proceeded to 53 CCS to take over charge took over charge of Ambulance from Lt Col Knocker D.S.O. Admitted 12. C.C.S.H. to duty 6. Remaining 27	
"	13/10/18		Admitted 6. C.C.S. 1. to duty 3. Remaining 29	
"	14/10/18		Admitted 5. duty 5. Remaining 29	
"	15/10/18		Admitted to officer 1. O.R. 1. C.C.S. 1 officer. to duty 4. Remaining 26	
"	16/10/18		Admitted 6. C.C.S. 6. to duty 10. Remaining 16	
"	17/10/18		Admitted 6. C.C.S. 13. to duty 9. Remains nil. Under W/O orders (55th Ade) Ambulance proceeded to D22.604. Personnel & kama in transit march. Transport by road.	

WAR DIARY or INTELLIGENCE SUMMARY

Army Form C. 2118

War Diary Ref. Sheet 57 B /unreadable/

Place	Date	Hour	Summary of Events and Information	Remarks and references to Appendices
TEMPLEUX LA FOSSE	18-10-18		Ambulance proceeded by route march to BEAUVOIR. Men though hard work caused by establishing and carrying out unit practice of Nissen standing. One case was to be clothing etc. The 9th evacuated to No 13. V.E.S.	SW Watts
BEAUVOIR	19-10-18		Ambulance by route march to ELINCOURT. Received orders that this Ambulance would take over Fromencountier during the Maurois's attack.	SW
ELINCOURT	20-10-18		Ambulance proceeded by unit march to MAUROIS.	SW
MAUROIS	21-10-18		Proceeded by unit march to REUMONT. Took over Fromencountier from 2/3 EAST LANCS Field Ambulance. Carried in conveyance of one 6 other ranks from A.D.S. in LE CATEAU. In the meantime opening an A.D.S. in REUMONT.	SW
REUMONT	22-10-18		Formed A.D.S. in LE CATEAU. Ambulance bearers transport moved to LE CATEAU. Were sworn attached to 73rd. also walking wounded post.	SW
LE CATEAU	23-10-18		Attack opened at 0120. See detailed statement of operations attached. SURGEON LT J D ARTHUR R.N. arrived relate. Casualties. Immense. 2. O.R. & evacuated. 1. O.R. Remained at duty.	SW
"	24-10-18		A.D.S. & Walking Wounded post opened in FOREST. The LE CATEAU A.D.S. closed at 2000. Casualties. 1. O.R. evacuated.	SW
FOREST	25-10-18		Transport moved from REUMONT to old A.D.S. LE CATEAU. Major J. H. CAMPBELL D.S.O. R.A.M.C. came over and took over command of Ambulance.	SW
"	26-10-18		Handed over command of Ambulance to Major J. A. CAMPBELL D.S.O. R.A.M.C. Situation Quiet. Admitted 17 S. 2 F.D. 9 evacuated to M.O.S.	Watts
"	27-10-18		Major Booth M.D. R.A.M.C. proceeded to W 139 F.A. for duty. Admitted 9 evacuated 21 W. 17 S.	J.H.C
"	28-10-18		Transferred A.D.S. to Bowers L.3 G.S.F. and opened at 15.00 Head of F.A. established in S. FOREST at Soldiers Home K.I.A. & O.R.'S	J.H.C
"	29-10-18		Admitted 26 S. 9 W. 1 Casualty N.S.(?) Pte Hitchcock R.A.M.C. (not evacuated)	J.H.C

Army Form C. 2118

WAR DIARY
or
INTELLIGENCE SUMMARY
(Erase heading not required.)

Instructions regarding War Diaries and Intelligence Summaries are contained in F. S. Regs., Part II. and the Staff Manual respectively. Title Pages will be prepared in manuscript.

Place	Date	Hour	Summary of Events and Information	Remarks and references to Appendices
FOREST	30.10.15		Admitted 2 9.S. 35-W. i evacuated. Major W.E. Hartgill M.C. R.A.M.C. reported from leave.	J.H.C.
"	31.10.15		Admitted 21 S. 35-W. i evacuated	J.H.C.

Operations 18 Division 23/10/18 to 27/10/18.

The Medical Arrangements during the Operations were as follows:

23/10/18.   A.D.S. LE CATEAU. K 34 a 4.2   (Map Refer. Sheet 57 B 1/10000.)
Relay Post. Square LE CATEAU.
Relay Post at 4 Valleys Cross Roads.

Right Sector. In the early part of the engagement the evacuation of this sector was carried out without difficulty by hand carry, both Stretcher Bearers and Prisoners being employed. It was not found possible to establish a Ford Car post in this sector until 07.00 as the situation was obscure. At this hour a car was placed at K 35 b 8.8. and at 10.00 it was found possible to move it forward to FARM du BOIS d' EOILLERS. L 25 a 2.3. At 13.00 the Ford Car Post was advanced to CORBEAU Farm L 25 a 7.8. and shortly after it was found practicable to move to FARM des TILLEURS L 16 a 3.2.

From this point the line of evacuation was changed to the FOREST route where large cars were now running down the ROMAN ROAD via MONTAY to the A.D.S. One large car was stationed at the FARM du Bois d' EOILLERS to deal with local casualties.

Left Sector. The Evacuation of this sector opened with hand carry to Relay Post in Square, LE CATEAU. At 04.00 a Ford Car post was established on the LE CATEAU – RICHMONT MILL Road at K 35 a 4.4, at 06.00 moved forward to the Railway embankment K 29 c 9.9., again moving forward at 08.00 to RICHMONT MILL. At this place it was found that the bridge over the River had not been repaired. As the aforementioned repair had not been effected at 11.00 Ford Cars were run via MONTAY to FOREST. – One Ford Car still being retained at RICHEMONT MILL until 16.00.

By 13.00 large cars were running to FOREST, K 12 d 4.6. and Ford Car was pushed on to CEMETERY, FOREST, L 7 c 9.9

24/10/18 The Evacuation of the whole division Front was now being effected on the one route – FOREST – RICHMONT MILL LE CATEAU Road. A Ford Car was pushed on to

(2)

(24/10/18 Continued)
BOUSIES L 3 c 6.9. An A.D.S. was established in FOREST at L.1 C.9.4 at 12.00, and the LE CATEAU A.D.S. continued to act until 20.00, when it closed.

25/10/18 The Ford Car Post was in the same position as yesterday. A second Ford Car Post was established at PAUL JAQUES FARM F.16.a.9.3. at 12.00. But had to be withdrawn for a short time owing to shelling. It was found possible to re-establish it however.

26/10/18. A large car post was established at 12.00 near HARPIES MILL F 21 c 8.9. The Evacuation on the right from ROBESART was to the FORD car post at F.29.c.4.4. and thence to large car post at HARPIES MILL; So that now all evacuation was down the main ROMAN Road to the A.D.S. at FOREST.

27/10/18 Arrangements continued as on 26th.
During the operations no delay or difficulty was experienced either in evacuation of cases from the line to the A.D.S., or from the A.D.S. to M.D.S.
The Motor Ambce. Cars from the three Field Ambces. were quite sufficient to deal with all stretcher cases. Three "Walking wounded" lorries were available on the 23rd, and it was found possible after mid-day on that date to dispense with 2 of these. On the 24th two lorries were asked for from M.A.C. and these cleared all W.W. cases in one journey returning to M.A.C. on completion of duty.
The following number of cases passed through the A.D.S:-

Period.	19 Div. S	19 Div. W	Other Troops S	Other Troops W	Prisoners S	Prisoners W	TOTAL S	TOTAL W
ZERO to noon 23/10/18	8	340	7	186		60	15	586
2a hours to noon 24th	10	118	7	59		20	17	197
- . - 25th	5	245	11	37		3	16	285
- . - 26th	13	95	5	20		nil	18	115
- . - 27th	14	21	3	7		1	17	29
Total.	50	819	33	309		84	83	1212

E.W.Booth.
Major R.A.M.C.
O.C. 55.1. Amb.

27.10.18.

140/3481

No. 5574 A

COMMITTEE FOR THE
MEDICAL HISTORY OF THE WAR
6 MAR 1919
Date

Nov. 1915

Army Form C. 2118

WAR DIARY or INTELLIGENCE SUMMARY

(Erase heading not required.) Maps—FRANCE 57 A/NE, 57 B/NW

Instructions regarding War Diaries and Intelligence Summaries are contained in F.S. Regs., Part II. and the Staff Manual respectively. Title Pages will be prepared in manuscript.

Place	Date	Hour	Summary of Events and Information	Remarks and references to Appendices
Le FOREST	1.11.18		No 7/3 024631 Pte Owen W. A.S.C. (H.T.) was killed by a shell in transport lines at Le CATEAU this morning at 03:15 hrs. The same shell wounded Pte 074 003415 D/vr Symonds J.H. ASC (H.T.) and killed 2 horses and wounded 2.	J. Hartgill Capt RAMC
"	2.11.18		a— Admitted 148 sick W & wounded	JATP
			A new site was chosen for an A.D.S. in BOUSIES F29 c 6.0 s. (Doctors House) Admitted 33 S, 29 W & evacuated	
	3.11.18		Handed over to Major Hartgill H.E.B. R.A.M.C. and proceeded to report to ADHS 23rd Div. Assumed temporary command of unit in accordance with XIII Corps ADMS A 865 of 2/11 J. Hartgill Capt. RAMC	K Hartgill
			Completed final arrangements and issued operation order to evacuation "" by same. Wounded of the Division. Copy of operation order attached Appendix 1.	K Hartgill
BOUSIES	4.11.18		Attack launched 06.15 hrs. An area captured including a Canal from Left Flank and the large car Post at PAUL JACQUES FARM were utilised as an A.D.S. and cars assisted direct to CMDS. Casualties have not been and all arrangements for evacuation kept smoothly. Shrapnel in PREUX was severe till after midday. A.D.S. was established in the village at A 20 b 81 with Post Car Post at A 22 b 3.9 before 4 p.m. and the post at PAUL JACQUES Farm withdrawn. A Large Car Post was Left at A 7 b 9.1.1 to clear any cases which still came down through HER8 from the Left Flank. H.Q. of the Amby was moved to BOUSIES early in the morning. 1168 Pte. MARIS C.E. RAMC. wounded and evacuated.	K.H.
	5.11.18		Attack continued. Large Car Post established at B 1 d central with Post Car Post at Le CROUSH INN B 10 c 9.6. Roads heavily congested with traffic making Evacuation very slow and laborious. By evening (owing to traffic congestion) large Car Post was established in hut at B 8 / a 2.6 and cars had to return to A.D.S. via ENGLEFONTAINE. Very few wounded – heavy rain all day – roads very difficult	

WAR DIARY
or
INTELLIGENCE SUMMARY

Army Form C. 2118

Maps. FRANCE 57 A / 1/40000
57 B
57 B

Place	Date	Hour	Summary of Events and Information	Remarks and references to Appendices
BOUSIES	5.11.18	(contd)	and met & forward work done by relays & bearers owing to impossibility of using Ford Cars about ROUTE du LANDRECIES forward of CADRE FOUR de L'HERMITAGE in B/14/d. 74627 Pte POULTON J.H. R.A.M.C. wounded and evacuated.	N/A
	6.11.18		A forward A.D.S. was established under cover at B 15 c 0.6 with Ford car Post at B 18 c 5.1 to clear cases from the R.A.P's at C 13 a 1.9 and C 7 c 2.0. Roads much too congested and evacuation easier in consequence. 56102 Pte DUNCAN A. R.A.M.C. been for wounded. Still raining.	hqs
	7.11.18		Stretcher cases from line - Flu. Aches. assembled with equipment at BOUSIES. Opened policinic at ROBERSART and PREUX. Numerous sick civilians attended and evacuated to hospital from these villages. Temp. Capt. MKA. RICHARDS M.C. appointed acting Major. 37265 Pte WOOD A.R. 75941 Pte SMART. D. awarded Military Medal for gallantry and devotion to duty in action. Auth. III Corps H.R. 18/30/18 d/29/10/18	N/A
POMMEREUIL	8.11.18		Moved to POMMEREUIL with 55 Inf. Bde. Group. Town very dirty and insanitary - numerous dead horses unburied.	N/A
"	9.11.18		Maj: W.C. HARTAILL M.C. awarded Bar to Military Cross. Auth. AMS. Fourth Army MS/H/11473 d/ 26.10.18. Remained closed.	N/A
"	10.11.18		Maj: J.H. CAMPBELL DSO. returned to take over Command of Unit.	N/A
"	11.11.18		Notification received of cessation of hostilities - armistice having been signed.	
"	12.11.18		Remained closed.	yokenfed
"	13.11.18		Marched out POMMEREUIL at 11.30 hrs. Arrived in ELINCOURT at 16.30 hours. Billeted Offic(and)Church (U.3 c 5.1)	do
ELINCOURT	14.11.18		Remained closed.	do
	15.11.18		do	

WAR DIARY or INTELLIGENCE SUMMARY

Army Form C. 2118

Place	Date	Hour	Summary of Events and Information	Remarks and references to Appendices
ELINCOURT	16.XI.18		Remained closed.	Officiating MO/FSE
"	17.XI.18		do	
"	18.XI.18		do	
"	19.XI.18		Salvage operations and general Sanitary measures within the village of ELINCOURT have been allotted to this unit and commenced to day	JMcE
			Major W.M. Richards M.C., R.A.M.C. and Capt. R.B. Stewart M.B., R.A.M.C. detailed to day to report to D.D.M.S. IX Corps for duty.	
"	20.XI.18		Remained closed. Work devoted towards Salvage and Sanitary operations within the village.	
"	21.XI.18		Preparation made for the carrying out of Educational Schemes.	
"	22.XI.18		Evacuations to C.C.S. from Brigade for week ending 23rd = 1 B. car.	
"	23.XI.18			
"	24.XI.18			
"	25.XI.18		Educational classes and lectures commenced.	
"	26.XI.18		Remained at rest.	
"	27.XI.18			
"	28.XI.18		Parade 13th Div. to practice for Inspection and March Past by Division.	JMcE
			1 Section under Capt Fring M.O.R.C., U.S.A. departed Moulin Seyoux LE CATEAU to take over building Occupied by No. 75 F.A. (25th Div.).	
"	29.XI.18		Remained at rest. Evacuations for week ending 30th = 1 Officer 3 2. O.R.	JMcE
"	30.XI.18		Educational classes have been arranged for between 9.00 hrs and 12.00 hrs. minute Sanitary Squad started, Routheny, Strathord, Cambrai, French, Accrington, and British, Trigonometry, Chemistry, Mathematics, Drawing, etc.	JMcE

140/3496

No 55 7 a

WAR DIARY
or
INTELLIGENCE SUMMARY

(Erase heading not required.)

Army Form C. 2118

Vol. # 2
55 F. AMB.

Place	Date	Hour	Summary of Events and Information	Remarks and references to Appendices
ELINCOURT	1·XII·15		Remained at Rest.	McCauley
"	2·XII·15		Review by 13th Division. Relvd by Major Gen. R.P. Lee. Lieut. A.C. Paterson R.A.M.C. reported for duty and posted to 2/Buffs.	
"	3·XII·15		Remained at Rest.	
"	4/XII/15		Under orders from A.D.M.S. 1st Div. Capt. A.E. HARRIMAN R.A.M.C. reported this F.A. for duty. He & Lieut. A.C. PATERSON R.A.M.C. took over duties as M.O. 2/8 rank. Authority A.Q. 45 2 M/12/26 of 8.12.15.	
"	5/XII/15		The King paid a visit to ELINCOURT yesterday at 12.00 hrs. and walked through the village.	
"	6/XII/15		Remained at rest. Surgeon Arthur H.N. transferred to 1/R.W. Kents & struck off strength. Evacuations for week = 32 o.r.	
"	7/XII/15		Brigade Rest Hospital Sqn Sy. Div Sick opened today in Grand Place, ELINCOURT.	
"	8·XII·15		4 Nurses transferred to Queens and prepared for railway journeys duties. Cpt. F.N. SKILTON R.A.M.C. reported for duty. Admitted to Det. H.A. Runnemy H.	
"	9·XII·15		3 Mules transferred to Cambrai for Demobilisation & struck off strength.	
"	10·XII·15		5/N. Lanc. Pioneers and 1/Queens turkey Regt. moved to VILLERS OUTREAUX today. M.O. Py. 2/R+P: T.15.a.5.6 and T.9.d.5.1. Admitted to Det. Hosp. 5 Runnemy 5. 1/Buffs, 5/8 Runney Regt. moved to new billets in MALINCOURT. Returned to Brigade Rest Hosp. 2 Runnemy 7	
"	12·XII·15		" " " 3 "	
"	13·XII·15			
"	14·XII·15		Lt W.F. Tindale R.A.M.C. reported for duty from Etaples. Capt T.B Cullen (General list) reported for duty as dentist and Capt Pheldon R.R.C. transferred to A.D.M.S.	

WAR DIARY or INTELLIGENCE SUMMARY

Army Form C. 2118

Vol. 42

55th F. Amb R

Place	Date	Hour	Summary of Events and Information	Remarks and references to Appendices
ELINCOURT	15.12.18		Brigade R.Hosp. admissions 1 remaining 7.	App.
	16.12.15		" " " " 1 " 8.	App.
	17.12.18		Casualties admitted to Brigade R.Hosp. from shell accident at 7th Buffs - 15. motley very severe wounds of legs all transferred to CCS. BUSIGNY	App.
	18.12.18		Brigade R.Hosp. admissions nil. Capt. T.B.CULLEN (Same Unit) returned to duty at 50 C.C.S.	App.
	19.12.18		Lieut. W.F.TISDALE proceeded to 85 Labour Group for duty. Capt. T. ASHTON. DAVIES joined this unit for duty from 85 Labour Group. Capt. R.D.BELL (Same Unit) reported for Temp. duty as dentist.	App.
			Military Population of Le Cateau are stated by the Commandant to number 4,000. Civil " " " " " " " " " " " 5,000. "Marie" to number 5,000. Capt. KING M.O.R.C. attends to all troops in area & assists the only civil doctor with the civil population.	
	20.12.18		Capt. T. ASHTON. DAVIES proceed to LE CATEAU to assist Capt. KING M.O.R.C.	App.
	21.12.18		Brigade R. Hosp. Admissions 2. O.R.	App.
	22.12.18		Nothing to Report.	App.
	23.12.18			
	24.12.18		Brigade R. Hosp. admissions 2. O.R.	
	25.12.18		No hospital - Xmas Day	App.
	26.12.18			
	27.12.18		admission to Brigade Ret. Hosp. - 1.	App.

Vol 422
55 F.A.mb

Army Form C. 2118

WAR DIARY
or
INTELLIGENCE SUMMARY
(Erase heading not required.)

Instructions regarding War Diaries and Intelligence Summaries are contained in F. S. Regs., Part II. and the Staff Manual respectively. Title Pages will be prepared in manuscript.

Place	Date	Hour	Summary of Events and Information	Remarks and references to Appendices
ELINCOURT	28.12.18		Brigade Rest. Hospital Admissions 1.	Appx
	29.12.18		" " " " 3	Appx
	30.12.18		" " " " 4	Appx
	31.12.18		" " " " 1	Appx

18 DIV

Box 174

No 65 Field ambulance

Army Form C. 2118

Vol. 43
55 F.A.H.B.

WAR DIARY
or
INTELLIGENCE SUMMARY
(Erase heading not required.)

Instructions regarding War Diaries and Intelligence Summaries are contained in F.S. Regs., Part II. and the Staff Manual respectively. Title Pages will be prepared in manuscript.

Place	Date	Hour	Summary of Events and Information	Remarks and references to Appendices
ELINCOURT	1-1-19		No hostilities. Advance to Brigade Rest Area B.	A/70. A/70.
"	2-1-19		" " " " " 2.	
"	3-1-19		Capt. & Quartermaster H.A. BROADBENT. R.A.M.C.(T) joined this unit for duty from D.D.M.S. BOULOGNE. BASE.	A/70
"	5-1-19		Lt. Col. J.W. Campbell returned to duty from leave & renewed command. D.D.M.S. 13th Corps (Col Dunn fr/FS) CMG/D visited & took over 75 Brigade Hospital. Admin ✓ 5 Evacuating 7.	Joseph T. Gen.
"	6-1-19		8th Northant Adm. ✓ tak Evac. 6.	pet
"	7-1-19		do " 1 " 7.	nbe
"	8-1-19		do " " "	pbe
"	9-1-19		do Adm in 2 "	gbe
"	10-1-14		do " " 9.	
"	11-1-19		do Adm 2 " 5.	
			Capt & Major W.C. Hartgill M.C. R.A.M.C. transferred from Establishment and struck off strength 3.1.19 Authority D.R. 113/704 of 6.1.19 General Parade of all ranks was held to-day and an address given by C.O. on the System to be carried out for Demobilisation. An allotment to 6 per Demobilisation has been received, one L/Col & 3 Pts 8th M.B.M. 1 Northant Adm. B. Bean 5.	A/pc
	12-1-19		defrosted to-day to BUSIGNY for Transfer to Corps Consolidation Camp. "3rd Northant Adm. B. Bean 5.	pc

WAR DIARY
or
INTELLIGENCE SUMMARY
(Erase heading not required.)

Army Form C. 2118
Vol 43
55 Fld Amb

Place	Date	Hour	Summary of Events and Information	Remarks and references to Appendices
ELINCOURT	13.1/19		Brigade Rest Hosp Oct – Nom. Y	JHE
	14/1/19		1 Pte proceeded to Corps Concentration Camp for Demobilisation	JHE
	15/1/19		Other PP. O.R. R.E. – 6th Rest Hosp. Q Punct 1 Nom J	JHE
	16/1/19		" " " " 2 " "	JHE
	17/1/19		" " " " Y 8 out place to Sidley (10th)	JHE
			An advance party despatched to-day to CAUDRY to take over billets there in accordance with Brigade Order.	JHE
	18/1/19		1 Man transferred to BUSIGNY for demobilisation. 1 A/Cpl and 2 men to BUSIGNY " " Orders received to proceed to CAUDRY have been rescinded and the unit is now under orders to transfer to LIGNY en-CAMBRESIS (O.R.B. Map 5713.) 1 N.C.O. and 12 men despatched as advance party. 1 A/Cpl and 2 men to CAUDRY for demobilisation 1 A.M.S and 1 Man to CAUDRY " "	JHE
On	19/1/19		The unit transferred to LIGNY-en-CAMBRESIS to-day.	JHE
LIGNY	20/1/19		1 Sgt. Maj and 2 men to CAUDRY for demobilisation	JHE
	21/1/19		4 Men to CAUDRY for demobilisation	
	22/1/19		Unit at rest in LIGNY.	JHE
	26/1/19		No further allotments for demobilisation received	JHE
	27/1/19		A031767 S/Maj H.R. Shelton A.A.M.C awarded the M.S.M. (L.G. Jan. 19, 25 Dec. 154/3955)	JHE

Army Form C. 2118

VOL 43 Jan a.
55 Jan a.

WAR DIARY
or
INTELLIGENCE SUMMARY

(Erase heading not required.)

Instructions regarding War Diaries and Intelligence
Summaries are contained in F. S. Regs., Part II.
and the Staff Manual respectively. Title Pages
will be prepared in manuscript.

Place	Date	Hour	Summary of Events and Information	Remarks and references to Appendices
LIGNY-en-Cambresis	28.I.19		Unit at rest in Ligny, with detachment at Le Cateau.	
"	30.I.19			
"	31.I.19			

110/3550

27 JUL 1919

SS/7a-

Apr 1919

WAR DIARY or INTELLIGENCE SUMMARY
(Erase heading not required.)

Army Form C. 2118

55TH FIELD AMBULANCE.

VOL. 46
LIGNY en CAMBRESIS
NORD FRANCE
Lt Col J.H. CAMPBELL RAMC

WO. 46

Place	Date	Hour	Summary of Events and Information	Remarks and references to Appendices
LIGNY	1-4-19		Unit closed. Preparations now in progress to bring equipment up to scale in accordance with new A.F. B 1095 – 120 (2 Section F.Amb mobilization Table).	
"	14-4-19		1 FfW transferred to CAMBRAI for demobilization. Office of A.D.M.S. 10th Div. Packet now transferred to this office.	
"	15-4-19		Major Burney RAMC DADMS reverts to regimental rank, & Capt. from 30/3/19 and taken on strength of 15th Divisional Packet for duty.	
"	16-4-19		Capt. Burney RAMC to command 41.C.C.S. earlier or to-day.	
"	17-4-19		Orders Administration thru (40th Coy Fd.) Packet now under ADMS No 3 Area, and orders issued through 88.M.O. 13 H.Co.Reg.) Group Packet.	
"	19-4-19		All horses now demobilised and 2 horses allotted from Divisional pool to be attached.	
"	29-4-19		Capt Daws MC, USA transferred from 56 F Amb. to American Head Qy. for demobilisation & sick and attached through Divisional Packet.	
"	30-4-19		Capt J Bellingham MC USA reported for duty and attached to 1050 F Amb.	

J Campbell
Lt Col RAMC

www.ingramcontent.com/pod-product-compliance
Lightning Source LLC
Chambersburg PA
CBHW081359160426
43193CB00013B/2066